CASE STUDIES IN
ARCHAEOLOGY SERIES

SERIES EDITOR
JEFFREY QUILTER
Ripon College

❑

Khok Phanom Di

Prehistoric Adaptation to the World's Richest Habitat

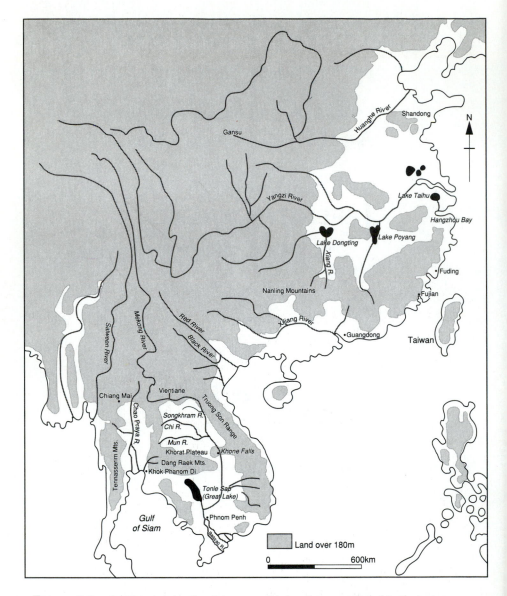

FIGURE 1.1   *Southeast Asia, showing geographic locations mentioned in the text.*

KHOK PHANOM DI

Prehistoric Adaptation to the World's Richest Habitat

Charles Higham
University of Otago
Dunedin, New Zealand

Rachanie Thosarat
Thai Fine Arts Department
Bangkok, Thailand

Harcourt Brace College Publishers
Fort Worth Philadelphia San Diego New York Orlando Austin San Antonio
Toronto Montreal London Sydney Tokyo

Publisher	Ted Buchholz
Acquisitions Editor	Christopher P. Klein
Developmental Editor	Linda Wiley
Project Editor	Annelies Schlickenrieder
Production Manager	Jane Tyndall Ponceti
Senior Book Designer	Serena Barnett Manning

ISBN: 0-15-500951-6

Library of Congress Catalog Card Number: 93-78496

Photo Credits: For permission to reproduce the photograph of a rice husk taken under an electronic microscope (Figure 4.3) the publisher is grateful to Jill Thompson and the Electron Microscope Unit of the Australian National University. The detailed drawing of a rice spikelet (Figure 4.4) was generously contributed by the International Rice Research Institute, Manila.

Address for Editorial Correspondence
Harcourt Brace College Publishers, 301 Commerce Street, Suite 3700, Fort Worth, TX 76102

Address for Orders
Harcourt Brace College Publishers, 6277 Sea Harbor Drive, Orlando, FL 32887
1-800-782-4479, or 1-800-433-0001 (in Florida)

Printed in the United States of America

3 4 5 6 7 8 9 0 1 2   067   0 9 8 7 6 5 4 3 2 1

For Tom, James, Emma,
Caroline, Joseph, and Petra

Foreword

ABOUT THE SERIES

These case studies in archaeology are designed to bring students, in beginning and intermediate courses in archaeology, anthropology, history, and related disciplines, insights into the theory, practice, and results of archaeological investigations. They are written by scholars who have had direct experience in archaeological research, whether in the field, laboratory, or library. The authors are also teachers, and in writing their books they have kept the students who will read them foremost in their minds. These books are intended to present a wide range of archaeological topics as case studies in a form and manner that will be more accessible than writings found in articles or books intended for professional audiences, yet at the same time preserve and present the significance of archaeological investigations for all.

ABOUT THE AUTHORS

Charles Higham has been Professor of Anthropology at the University of Otago, New Zealand, since 1968. He was educated at Raynes Park Grammar School, London, and St. Catharine's College, Cambridge. He graduated in 1962 with a double first, and went on to complete his Ph.D. there on the later prehistory of Denmark and Switzerland. In 1966, he was appointed lecturer in archaeology at the University of Otago, and began his fieldwork in Southeast Asia two years later. He has returned to undertake further excavations at regular intervals.

He has always stressed the importance of working with Thai colleagues, and many have joined him in the field and then for their research degrees in New Zealand. After a period of collaboration with Chester Gorman at Ban Chiang and Spirit Cave, he co-directed the excavation of Ban Na Di in 1981, published in 1984 with Amphan Kijngam, and in 1984–85, he worked with Rachanie Thosarat at Khok Phanom Di. The first three volumes of their report have been published, and there are four more to come. Their most recent excavation at Nong Nor is now entering its fourth season and is the largest area uncovered in a prehistoric Thai site.

Charles Higham is on the editorial board of *Antiquity*, the *Holocene*, and the *Journal of Archaeological Science* and is a committee member of the Indo-Pacific Prehistory Association. He is a fellow of the Society of Antiquaries of London, and of the Royal Society of New Zealand, and a former fellow of St. John's College, Cambridge. He has given lectures at Harvard, Yale, and the University of Pennsylvania, where he was for many years a research affiliate.

He is married, with two sons and two daughters. His oldest son is specializing in radiocarbon dating, and has been responsible for dating the site of Nong Nor.

Rachanie Thosarat met Charles Higham in 1975, when both were involved in the excavation of Ban Chiang. She took her first degree in archaeology at Silpakon University, Bangkok, before going to the University of Pennsylvania to study for her M.Sc. She is a research officer with the Fine Arts Department in Bangkok, which has involved her in many excavations in Thailand.

In 1984, she became co-director of the Bang Pakong Valley research program, and joined Charles Higham in an initial site survey, followed by the excavation of Khok Phanom Di. With a Ford Foundation scholarship, she then undertook her doctoral dissertation in Otago on the social organization represented by the mortuary data from the site.

In 1989, she returned to her post in Bangkok, and has since co-directed the excavation of Nong Nor. For two seasons, she has also directed excavations at Ban Chiang in northeast Thailand. She is widely regarded for her meticulous excavation technique and sharp eye in the field.

ABOUT THIS CASE STUDY

As the second book in our case studies series, *Khok Phanom Di* is welcome for a great number of reasons. For the purposes of providing students with an example of how archaeology is done and to what ends, no better example can be found than this account of work conducted in Thailand. Charles Higham and Rachanie Thosarat's coverage of everything from the initial discovery of the site, to seeking funding, through the excavations, to the final analyses of materials provides ample material for class discussions and lectures.

The site is a marvel. It has remarkable preservation given its tropical locale, and the information available on mortuary customs is among the best there is, anywhere. The meticulous excavations and the careful analyses, described so well in this book, are exemplars in the field of prehistoric archaeology. Such work was done with care, but also with vigor and great imagination. It is not every research project that can boast the recovery of genealogical links between several generations of burials *and* the discovery of the world's oldest wind chimes!

Equally important as the pedagogical merits of this work is its value as a contribution from Southeast Asia. Given that the majority of archaeologists who will use the case studies series volumes in their classes also define themselves as anthropologists, a truly crosscultural comparison of sites, methods, and theories is in order in archaeology classes. Too often, however, many third world regions are placed in the back of archaeology textbooks, never to be reached because the semester ends before the text is finished. In addition, the specialization of graduate training often results in professional archaeologists with very little knowledge of prehistory outside a narrow geographical band. Too often, a provincialism develops, so that some regions are discounted altogether as unworthy of serious study. Case studies such as this one should help contribute to providing alternative examples of prehistoric cultures that are not adequately covered in other formats. Books such as this one will provide professors the opportunity of taking a chance at discussing something different and perhaps even adding to their own knowledge of world archaeology.

The authors' discussion of the larger context by which *Khok Phanom Di* can be appreciated is thus especially welcome because it will help instructors and students alike to better understand the important regional archaeological questions addressed in conducting the work. But *Khok Phanom Di* does not stand isolated. Many of the specific topics presented in the volume have direct bearing on larger issues found elsewhere, such as the role of marine resources, the spread of agriculture, and social archaeology, to name but a few, and the authors clearly explain how their research in Thailand fits into general concerns of archaeology throughout the world.

I have enjoyed reading about the exciting work and discoveries at *Khok Phanom Di* and in the larger culture region. I am confident that the readers of this book will also benefit and appreciate the rich account provided by its authors.

Jeffrey Quilter

Series Editor
Ripon, Wisconsin

Preface

Archaeology came late to Thailand, so every site excavated represents a major increase in our knowledge. This new information, however, must be shared to be of any lasting importance. We met during the excavation of Ban Chiang in 1975, and our subsequent collaboration in the field has now involved the excavation of Khok Phanom Di, which is the subject of this book, and of Nong Nor, which after three seasons now incorporates an area of 400 square meters. Our intention in writing this book is to share our discoveries at Khok Phanom Di, to describe our plans, hopes, discoveries, and growing appreciation of the people of this site as they unfolded. We would also like to try to place the site into its broader, regional perspective. Since preparations for the excavation and the writing of parts of the final report took place when we were half a world apart, the first person is used in certain parts of the text below to cover planning and other aspects of the research undertaken by Charles Higham.

Central Thailand has been the subject of much archaeological research recently, and it is now possible to perceive the broad outline of the cultural sequence. All dates mentioned for prehistoric sites are in calibrated years B.C. Initially, there were two major forms of adaptation, one in the uplands to the moist, canopied forest and the other on the coast, where the inhabitants took advantage of the natural wealth of the marine resources. Khok Phanom Di represents a late stage in the latter area. Located on an estuary between 2000–1500 B.C., its inhabitants collected the natural bounty of the shore and mangroves, cultivated rice, made pottery vessels, and exchanged local for exotic goods while at the same time, they had to cope with health problems. Many infants died at or soon after birth.

The research undertaken by the University of Pennsylvania team under the direction of Vincent Pigott has added a new dimension to our understanding of the beginning and nature of metal working. Just over 100 kilometers to the north of Khok Phanom Di, the Khao Wong Prachan Valley was a focus for copper working from about 1500 B.C. His sites, in particular Non Pa Wai, evidence the whole gamut of metal working, from mining the copper to ore dressing, smelting, and casting. No tin was used, for the ores were naturally rich in arsenic. At nearby Nil Kham Haeng, iron made its appearance about 600 B.C. There is little room for doubt that these intial dates also represent indigenous developments. There is no evidence of an introduction from outside.

Not long after iron came on stream, we find major changes in social organization, which involved the establishment of large settlements, along with evidence for the exchange of goods with Indian merchants. By the beginning of the first millennium A.D., some of these centers were taking on the characteristics of early states. Inscriptions were erected, employing texts which inform us that the local languages included Mon and Khmer, ancestral to those still spoken in the area. Both these belong to the Austro-Asiatic family, and have no known affiliations with the Chinese family of languages to the north. There are thus strong grounds for supposing that the achievements of the prehistoric people of Southeast Asia, which were many, represent a broad continuum down to the present.

Working in Southeast Asia has been a privilege for us both, and deeply rewarding. If any of this feeling is conveyed to and shared by the reader, one of our major objectives will have been achieved.

ACKNOWLEDGMENTS

We wish to acknowledge help from many quarters, all of which has contributed to making this book possible. The Fine Arts Department under the direction of Taweesak Sennanarong provided the permission to excavate, and Pisit Charoenwongsa was at all times encouraging and supportive. The necessary financial support was made available by the Ford Foundation, the Wenner Gren Foundation, Earthwatch and its Research Corps, The British Academy, the University of Cambridge through the Evans Fund, and the University of Otago. Support in the field was provided by Anat Bamrungwongse, Judith Brown, Phrapid Choosiri, Diane Hall, Thomas Higham, Amphan Kijngam, Bernard Maloney, Damrongkiadt Noksakul, Jacqui Pilditch, Pirapon Pisnupong, Glen Standring, Jill Thompson, and Brian Vincent. Without the assistance of the Abbot of Wat Khok Phanom Di and the many people who worked with us, the excavation would never have commenced.

Many colleagues and students have contributed to the analysis and publication of the material recovered, the list of names being too long to include, but their contributions will be evident from reading the book. Jeffrey Quilter has been supportive at all times, while Ruth Daniel kindly read and commented on the typescript.

Finally, Charles Higham acknowledges the kindness and encouragement of the Master and Fellows of St. John's College, Cambridge, for electing him one of their number in 1991–92, and for providing the facilities, academic and collegial, for sitting down and writing.

Contents

1
Introduction

◼

This book examines an episode in the human settlement of the world's richest habitat. The events to be described took place over five centuries, starting about 2000 B.C., at the mouth of a large river as it entered the Gulf of Siam in Thailand. During those five hundred years, the site, known as Khok Phanom Di, grew to a height of 12 meters above the surrounding terrain, and ultimately covered about 5 hectares. Khok Phanom Di can be translated from the Thai as the "Good Mound." It is a prominent feature in a landscape dominated by flat rice fields. It was once located at the mouth of an estuary, but the sea is now 22 kilometers to the west as the crow flies. Reaching the site is straightforward, for the main road east from Bangkok takes you almost to the doorstep in an hour.

Southeast Asia has no prescribed boundaries, and for the purposes of this book, we will use the term to encompass the area from the valleys of the Yangzi to the Chao Phraya rivers (Fig. 1.1). This area includes the southern part of the modern state of China, Vietnam, Cambodia, Laos, and Thailand.

The natural wealth of this area has been matched, until recently, by an almost complete ignorance of its prehistoric past. Its extensive low-lying alluvial plains produce a high proportion of the world's rice. The broad continental shelves sustain a great density of fish, augmented by the deltas and mangrove shores on the coast and the extensive inland lakes. Southeast Asia has extensive sources of copper and until recently, supplied almost 90 percent of the world's tin. Iron ore is widely available. The area still contains the world's largest religious complex built at Angkor.

These features alone are sufficient to fuel an interest in the area's prehistoric past. But as the number of excavations has grown during the last two decades, the cultural innovations that are unfolding increasingly demand attention. We know, for example, that rice cultivation had its origins in Southeast Asia (perhaps more than once) and that it was the springboard for the expansion of human societies into island Southeast Asia, across the Pacific to South America and westward, ultimately to Madagascar. We are increasingly coming to appreciate that Central Thailand was one of the few regions that witnessed the origins of copper-working and the alloying of copper with tin to produce bronze. Iron is widespread and the forging of iron tools also

1

seems to have had indigenous origins. Khok Phanom Di belongs to the period when human populations were growing and agricultural communities were being established, but before bronze was widely available. Its inhabitants cultivated rice, but although copper was probably already being worked in the Khao Wong Prachan valley to the north, no metal goods reached Khok Phanom Di. This site also produced an unparalleled variety of biological remains when compared to other Southeast Asian settlements, and it has been possible to assemble a team of scientists in many disciplines, all sharing the common goal of illuminating how this prehistoric society functioned within its rich but changeable coastal habitat.

Both in terms of its prehistoric past and its present environment, it is possible to identify features that give Southeast Asia individuality. All of the lowland terrain, for example, is affected by the monsoon, providing a sharp distinction between wet and dry seasons. The impact of the monsoon, particularly the difficult dry season, is lessened if one has access to the sea, because marine resources do not rely on the rains for survival. This is also a region where wild rice was once widely distributed and in which cultivated rice today sustains a dense lowland population. Now in excess of seven hundred million, it represents about one sixth of humanity. The present inhabitants are nearly all southern Mongoloid in terms of racial stock, but speak a myriad of languages. These are divided into three language families, the Austro-Tai, Austro-Asiatic, and Sino-Tibetan. The present distribution of these languages has a considerable bearing on the pattern of human cultural development, which will be discussed below. Similarly, the area was affected by a sudden and dramatic rise in sea level. Following the end of the Pleistocene Ice Age, glacial meltwater led to a rapid rise in the sea level. Nowhere was this more keenly felt than in Southeast Asia, due to the extensive, flat continental shelves (Fig. 1.2). These formerly broad plains, crossed by the ancestors of the modern truncated rivers, would have been fringed by deep belts of mangrove. By between 6000 and 4000 years B.C., the sea had risen higher than its present level and formed shorelines still discernible behind the modern coast. It is on one of these shorelines that Khok Phanom Di is situated.

In describing this area, we will begin with the rivers. Their distribution resembles the spokes of a wheel, with the hub located in the eastern margins of the Himalayas. For several hundred miles the headwaters of the Salween, Mekong, and Yangzi follow a parallel course only a few miles apart before they go their separate ways. Where the Yangzi and Mekong bifurcate, the Red River begins. The Xijiang has its origins in the uplands of Yunnan. The Chao Phraya was once one of the longest rivers of Southeast Asia, but the rise in sea level during the Holocene inundated its middle and lower reaches. Nevertheless, it drains a considerable catchment area, which includes highlands to the north, east, and west. It flows through a broad, flat plain, much of which accumulated as the river burst its banks during the rainy season and laid down silt deposits. Even as recently as a century ago, this plain was sparsely inhabited, a flat wasteland of marshes and stunted trees, mosquito-infested and difficult to cross. The construction of canals to drain the marshes and improve transport transformed the situation. Settlers

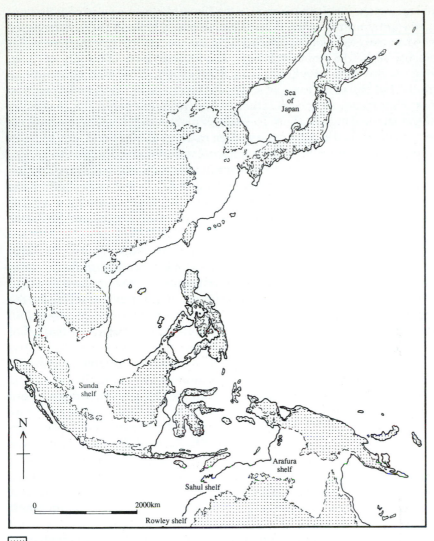

FIGURE 1.2 *Southeast Asia during the height of the last glacial period (about 16,000 years ago), showing the extent of the area which was later to be inundated by the rising sea.*

moved down the new waterways, founding communities, and by degrees brought the land under cultivation (Hanks 1972). Three smaller rivers also empty into the upper Gulf of Siam, each providing access by lowland people to the stone and mineral resources of the hinterland.

This area, known as the Bangkok Plain, is separated from other river systems by uplands, which have historically divided the peoples of Southeast Asia. Henri Mouhot, the French naturalist who explored Siam in the nineteenth century, provides a clear reflection of this in his diaries (Mouhot 1864). Crossing the plain by river was straightforward, but disembarking and traveling by elephant over the Petchabun Range to the Khorat Plateau was grindingly slow, difficult, and uncomfortable. When Mouhot finally crossed the mountains, he reached an elevated plateau drained from the west to the east by three major rivers, the Mun, Chi, and Songkhram. The first two meet at the city of Ubon, having crossed their own floodplains. The Songkhram initially flows to the northeast, but arcs to the east and south and finally flows into the Mekong. The Khorat Plateau has long been rather remote from the political heartland of Thailand on the Bangkok Plain. The eastern margin is defined by the Mekong River, which originates high in the eastern margins of the Himalayas. Much of its upper course cuts through precipitous uplands, forming impressive gorges, but below the capital of Laos at Vientiane, it enters a flatter landscape. Its passage is interrupted again at the Khone Falls before it proceeds south of the Dang Raek Range into Cambodia. At Phnom Penh, four waterways meet. The Mekong divides into two channels to the sea, the main stream and the Bassac branch.

Above the junction, the Tonle Sap River links the Mekong with the Great Lake, or Tonle Sap. In 1296, Chinese envoys took this route on their way to Angkor. The Dutch merchant Geritt van Wuystoff traveled up the Mekong to Laos in the early seventeenth century, and in 1866 a French team under the leadership of Captain Doudart de Lagree traveled up the Mekong deep into southern China. There they crossed the watershed into the upper reaches of the Red River.

The Red River flows from Yunnan to the Gulf of Bac Bo (Tonkin), passing in the main through precipitous uplands, and only reaching the flat deltaic landscape at Viet Tri and its confluence with the Black River. It bears a very heavy silt load, hence its name, and the delta is advancing rapidly. The Mekong and Red river systems are separated by the rugged Truong Son Cordillera, known to the Chinese as the "Fortress of the Sky." This range marks the maximum southern extent of Chinese imperial expansion.

The humid tropics, which characterize the lowlands of the Red, Mekong, and Chao Phraya valleys, continue to about 23 degrees north, although it must be remembered that, during the Holocene climatic optimum about seven thousand years ago, the climate was warmer and the tropical habitat may well have reached into the Xijiang River Valley. This valley attracts abundant monsoon rains, which support evergreen forests. The deltaic lowlands of the Xijiang River represent one of the most bountiful farming systems known. The mean temperature in the coldest month does not fall below 13 degrees Celsius, and the rainfall, at more than 1600 millimeters per annum, is more than sufficient for rice cultivation. As one proceeds in an easterly direction to the hilly coastal region of eastern Guangdong and Fujian, however, the coastal plain narrows, and there is a series of smaller deltaic areas that support population concentrations. The coastal vegetation in this area continues to be dominated by mangrove species, the northernmost extent of which lies at Fuding, 27 degrees 20 minutes north, although mangroves would have extended much further to the north during the warmer conditions that prevailed seven thousand years ago.

North of the fertile Xijiang Valley, we encounter the Nanling Mountains, which divide southern from central China over a north–south extent of 400 kilometers. These uplands are highest to the west, with peaks of over 2000 meters clothed in subtropical evergreen forest. The uplands, however, are not impenetrable. Access between the two major regions is possible via the Xianjiang corridor, which links the Xijiang with the Lake Dongting region of the middle Yangzi, and the Ganjiang, which provides access to the Lake Poyang region to the north. Both these lake systems, which were formerly much more extensive, lie in the middle Yangzi Valley. This profoundly important area, in historic terms, lies within the humid subtropics. Songquiao (1986) has identified three definitive characteristics of the middle and lower Yangzi valleys: the area has a mean air temperature in January of over freezing and receives over 750 millimeters of rainfall per annum. Natural vegetation is dominated by broad-leaved evergreen forest. Rice is the staple, and water is the principal means of communication. The middle and lower reaches of this river comprise a series of extensive valley plains. In the middle section from Yichang to Wuhan lies the Yunmeng swamp region, Lake Dongting being the biggest of many lakes. Now a shadow of its previous extent, it is surrounded by rich lacustrine alluvial soils which provide evidence for its former size. After a more constricted valley section, the river plain opens up to include Lake Poyang, now one of China's largest, and again above the delta, we encounter Lake Taihu, formerly a shallow arm of the sea during the Holocene high sea level. This valley system enjoys a hot summer climate and abundant rain. The "Plum Rains" of June usually bring heavy and continuous precipitation, which is ideal for the young rice plants (Domrös and Gongbing 1988).

Whichever climatic classificatory system is employed, we find continuity over the huge area from the Chao Phraya to the Yangzi characterized by the summer monsoon. This distinction between a wet and a dry season is the result of wind shifts, which respond to the changes in atmospheric pressure over the East Asian landmass. Low pressure there during the hot summers draws air from the southwest, but during the winter, the wind flow reverses and cool air moves from the northeast. In Southeast Asia, the impact of this reversal varies with locality and altitude, but in general a humid wet season lasts from May to November, and a dry season begins in December and ends in late April or early May. On the Khorat Plateau, where there are rainshadow effects during both seasons, the dry season is prolonged and harsh. To the east of the Truong Son Range, however, there is more cloud cover and some rain, and the dry season is less intense. The uplands also attract more rain than the inland plains. During the wet season, rains come in the form of brief but intense storms, and the rivers soon fill to overflowing. This is particularly serious in the case of the Mekong and Yangzi, whose flow is also augmented by the melting snow in the Himalayas. The former carries so much water that the flow of the Tonle Sap River is reversed and water from the Mekong reaches as far as the Great Lake of Cambodia. The Mun also chokes at its confluence with the Mekong, and widespread flooding ensues. Even in its lower reaches, the Mekong and Bassac spread widely across the flat landscape. There is so much rainfall in the Yangzi catchment that eight of its tributaries have a greater annual flow of water than the Huanghe to the north. The Yangzi itself has an annual flow of 979.35 billion cubic meters of water, depositing 450 million cubic meters of silt at the delta each year.

The plants and animals of Southeast Asia have to adapt to this sharp seasonal variation. Trees in the lowland forests, for example, are in the main deciduous, shedding their leaves in the dry season. Some fish have adapted to the desiccation of their habitat by sinking into the soft mud and living immobile until the rains return. Many shellfish burrow into the soil to aestivate, returning to breed only with the next wet season. Human groups have to store the food surpluses of the wet season to survive the dry. Rice, and fish fermented with salt, are the staples in this strategy. As one climbs in altitude, however, there are subtle but important changes in the vegetation. This reflects the higher rainfall experienced in the mountains. At 400 meters, the deciduous forest gives way to more evergreen species. By 1000 meters in altitude in areas with over 2000 millimeters of rain a year, canopied rainforests develop.

The impact of the monsoon, with its difficult dry season, is hardly felt at such altitudes. Its effect is also greatly reduced for those living in lacustrine or coastal regions. Lack of rainfall does not affect the fish, shellfish, or mangrove food resources, for they rely on the sea for their energy. Lakes are a different matter, because they are affected so much by river flows. The edge of the Tonle Sap, for example, moves over many kilometers, endangering local inhabitants with flooding for part of the year and with difficulty of access during the rest.

Human settlement harmonizes in many respects with this environmental mosaic. The canopied upland rainforests present several sources of food. There are the fruits and nuts of the trees and shrubs themselves, fish and shellfish from the permanent streams, and the animals that are adapted, in the main, to an arboreal life. We find the remains of prehistoric activity in rock shelters, and these invariably reveal temporary occupation by small groups of people. This is hardly surprising, given the low concentrations of food in any given locality. Most animals, for example, are small and arboreal, adapted to eating the fruits and leaves of the canopy. Plant foods are localized and seasonal.

This situation is in marked contrast to the lowlands, where the monsoon is keenly felt, and lakes, rivers, and swamps provide not only for the cultivation of rice in their margins, but also for a steady supply of wet-season fish. This habitat, once brought under cultivation, is one of the richest agricultural ecosystems in the world. Archaeologically, it is also one of the least known, and the archaeological research at Khok Phanom Di was designed to throw some light on the origins and development of an agricultural system that now sustains a high percentage of the human race.

THE ARCHAEOLOGICAL SEQUENCE

We know that small bands of hunter-gatherers occupied part of Southeast Asia well back into the Pleistocene Period. In the uplands flanking the Red River, Vietnamese archaeologists have identified about sixty sites which they ascribe to the Son Vi culture. This culture belongs to the period from at least 18,000 to 11,000 B.C. Anderson (1990) has found even earlier hunter-gatherer contexts at the large cave of Lang Rongrien, dated to at least 35,000 years B.C.

A later adaptation to the upland habitat, dated from about 11,000–3,000 B.C., has been identified in many parts of the region. In the rugged karst landscape flanking the Red River floodplain, for example, numerous rock shelters have been excavated. These are usually located so as to give access to freshwater resources. The material culture of these people, who have for long been known under the term Hoabinhian after the Vietnamese province in which they were first recognized, includes a limited range of stone artifacts and several tool types made of bone. There is also a strong likelihood that they used wood a great deal, but this evidence has not survived. Local river cobbles were flaked, on one side only, to form what was probably a multipurpose chopping tool. Others were flaked into the shape of an axe, or into pointed implements. Points and awls were fashioned from bone. An innovation common in the hilly country north of the Red River was the grinding and polishing of adzes. This technique provides a much more efficient cutting implement, particularly when it is hafted to a wooden handle. Some of the upper layers of these rock shelters also contain the remains of pottery vessels.

Similar sites have been found in the provinces of southern China, in Cambodia and Thailand. Indeed, for many years virtually any site containing a similar stone technology to that identified in northern Vietnam was named Hoabinhian. Heijinglong in the headwaters of the Xijiang, for example, is a rock shelter which has a series of ash layers in association with the remains of deer, bear, cattle, and macaque bones. At Xijiaoshan, on the margins of the Xijiang delta plain, there are several open sites characterized by a flaked stone technology, with no evidence for pottery or the polishing of stone tools.

Perhaps the best-known group of such rock shelters was examined by Chester Gorman between 1966–72. Spirit, Banyan Valley, and Steep Cliff caves are located in the uplands of northern Thailand. For the first time in such sites, Gorman passed the cultural deposits through a fine screen, and was rewarded with the recovery of plant remains. Spirit Cave, which was sporadically occupied between about 11,000 and 5,500 B.C., has yielded the remains of numerous varieties of plants. Some, such as the Chinese water chestnut (*Trapa*), are edible. Others are known for their use as poisons to aid hunting. Still others, such as the betel nut (*Areca*), have narcotic properties. The screening procedure also supplied a sample of microfauna. There are the remains of small squirrels, the marten, and civets, each representing the forest canopy. Ground-dwelling animals were also hunted or trapped, including the porcupine, badger, and leopard cat. Some larger deer were present, but big mammals were relatively rare. This is not surprising, given that the site is located at 650 meters above sea level on the edge of a precipitous slope. It is a sharp climb to reach it from the Khong Stream in the valley floor, but some fish, crabs, and shellfish were taken up there.

The surface of Layer 2 at the top of the deposit revealed a series of intriguing artifacts: 426 shards of pottery, some polished stone adzes, and small ground-edged slate knives. Gorman claimed that these date to about 6000 B.C., and if this were true, it would have major implications for our understanding of the prehistoric societies in this part of Thailand as well as more generally. This observation reflects the common association between pottery and sedentary communities. Moreover, the small knives reminded

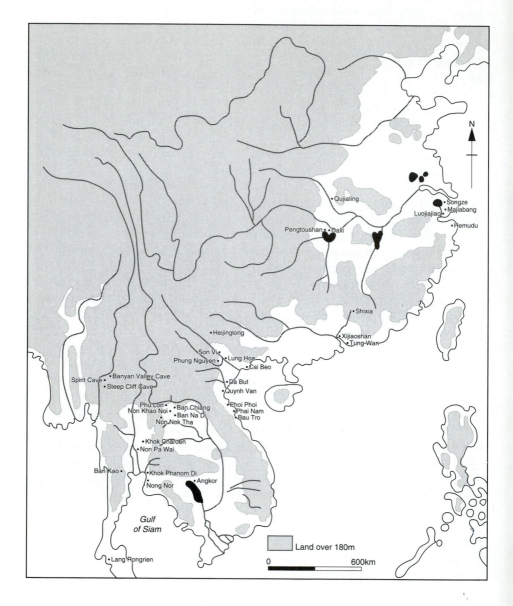

FIGURE 1.3   *Southeast Asia, showing prehistoric sites mentioned in the text.*

Gorman of Indonesian rice-harvesting implements. This new set of artifacts might, therefore, have been associated with some form of plant cultivation. However, no plant remains from this site qualify as domesticates.

In 1972, Gorman expanded his search for evidence that plant cultivation might have had its origins in the uplands of northern Thailand. He was taken to a large series of caverns adjacent to a stream as it cascades into a swallow-hole in the adjacent hillside. A small test excavation at Banyan Valley Cave revealed stone implements just like those from Spirit Cave, much ash and evidence for hearths, and the same presence of pottery and polished stone adzes as in the upper levels. More intriguing still were the remains of rice husks.

A large excavation followed in December 1972, and the sequence was confirmed. Fine screening of the cultural deposits likewise yielded a range of plants similar to those from Spirit Cave, in association with 110 rice husks. Clearly, the possibilities posed by the Spirit Cave dates could be confirmed by the analysis of the status of the rice from Banyan Valley and its date. Yen (1977), in a meticulous study employing 128 modern comparative varieties of rice, concluded that the prehistoric remains come from a wild variety. When the dates were obtained, it was found that, while the lowest levels at the cave belong to about 3500 B.C., the upper ones containing the rice and pottery are much later, falling in the first millennium A.D.

Numerous rock shelter sites like those examined by Gorman indicate a widespread distribution of small, upland groups of foragers. Similar sites have been found in the rugged interior drained by the Xijiang River, and in the hills surrounding the Bangkok Plain. There was, however, a further aspect to the settlement of Southeast Asia from the period when a higher sea level involved the formation of new coastal conditions. Both in southern China and north to central Vietnam, there are numerous prehistoric sites from which marine resources were exploited. Tung Wan in Hong Kong is one such site. Layer 4 there, which probably dates between 4000–3000 B.C., contained a series of stone tools based on flaking cobbles, which recall those found in the upland rock shelters. Pottery was also found, the shards being tempered with sand. No evidence for domestication of any plant or animal species other than the dog has been found, but clearly fishing was important. In Layer 3, there were a number of changes in the stone tool industry, including the presence of polished stone adzes and of grinding stones, probably used to sharpen the adze heads. This layer, dated from 3000 B.C., also provides no evidence for agriculture, although the analysis of human remains suggests that a high proportion of the diet came from plant remains (Qiao Xiaoqin 1991). The presence of lagoons behind such sites as Tung Wan could have provided an environment suited to rice cultivation, although the actual evidence is wanting.

This pattern of sedentary coastal settlement is also encountered in Vietnam. Cai Beo, Da But, and Quynh Van, settlements in the northern part of the country, were founded not long after the new coast was established. At Da But, for example, a radiocarbon date in the vicinity of 5000 B.C. has been obtained. Excavations there also recovered polished stone adzes and much pottery. The former are similar to those found in some of the rock shelters in the uplands behind the coastal plain. Cai Beo, on the island of Cat Ba, is also important in yielding in its basal layer a stone tool industry reminiscent of the inland Hoabinhian rock shelters. This layer is dated to the fifth millennium B.C., and was followed by a layer containing the same polished stone adzes and incised and cord-marked pottery. Pottery was also found at Da But, Bau Tro, Quynh Van, Phoi Phoi, and Phai Nam. The last two sites also contained large stone hoes. These, along with the polished stone adzes and pottery remains, have encouraged Vietnamese archaeologists to suggest that plant cultivation was practised in these coastal sites. This might well be true, but can be determined only by future recovery and analysis of the plant remains themselves, for hoes can just as easily be used to obtain wild as domesticated plants. These sites do, nevertheless, illuminate several important points. The occupants of inland rock shelters were contemporaneous with sedentary coastal groups which displayed a similar stone industry, but also much pottery. The origins of these coastal communities, it is suggested, probably lie on the now inundated continental shelves. They are considered the most likely source for the technological innovations in the rock shelters because, while occupation in the shelters was clearly intermittent, the coast is more likely to have attracted permanent, sedentary communities in which a range of new types of artifact, such as pottery, could have been employed. When such early coastal sites were examined, they revealed a considerable depth of cultural material, and communal cemeteries. As yet, however, there is no convincing evidence of the cultivation of domesticated plants in the Vietnamese sites.

Identifying the transition to rice cultivation is a central issue in the prehistory of Southeast Asia. Rice is adapted in nature to freshwater swamps, and is therefore to be found where monsoon rains or permanent lakes provide suitable conditions. Wild rice seeds are difficult to harvest, unless they are beaten into a boat or basket, because the slightest touch leads to shattering of the rachis and seed dispersal. The period of seed maturation is also brief, and its timing is uneven. A harvester may, therefore, find that only a small proportion of the seeds are ripe and many will be lost as they are collected. However, by seed selection in favor of varieties with more even ripening qualities and a stronger rachis, rice becomes one of the most productive crops known. A widespread characteristic of the early cultivation of grains is the opportunity it provides for an increase in human population, and their expansion into new territories.

Considerable advances have recently been made in understanding the origins of rice cultivation in Southeast Asia. A series of village sites has been identified in the middle and lower reaches of the Yangzi River, sites which have yielded considerable quantities of rice remains and agricultural implements. The earliest, Pengtoushan, is located near the northern shore of Lake Dongting in the middle valley of the Yangzi (Fig. 1.1). The radiocarbon dates suggest occupation between about 6500–5800 B.C., a time when a long period of increasing warmth was followed by rather cooler conditions. Marshes and lakes of this region were considerably more extensive than at present, and wild rice is thought to have flourished. Wild floating rice is still to be found in Anhui Province. At Pengtoushan, we encountered a new settlement configuration, a mound that covered a hectare and ultimately rose to a height of 4 meters. Excavations in 1988 revealed the remains of houses and a cemetery. Some burials contained rice chaff-tempered pottery vessels as offerings and small stones which might have been used for removing the husks from rice. Diagnosing such remains as coming from a wild or a domestic source is very difficult, often impossible. Essentially, one needs access to the awns, the process that grows at the end of the seed, and the point of attachment to the stalk, before definite conclusions are possible, for both respond to the process of domestication. Therefore, we must suspend judgement on the status of the Pengtoushan rice. It may have been collected from wild stands along the margins of Lake Dongting. Certainly, none of the agricultural implements found in later sites, such as spades and sickles, have been found there.

Later sites in this area, however, are more easily interpreted as being engaged in rice farming. The Daxi culture, for example, dated between 4500 and 3000 B.C., incorporates a considerable number of sites in which rice remains are abundant, as well as stone spades and shell and stone reaping-knives. These villages had houses, storage pits, and cemeteries, and were clearly occupied over long periods. The excavations at the cemetery of Daxi, for example, have provided 208 inhumation graves accompanied by a variety of grave goods. Jade, ivory, and shell ornaments reveal a growing exchange in exotic jewelry. This culture was succeeded by the Qujialing (3000–2500 B.C.), again based on rice cultivation. Many artifacts develop out of Daxi forms, and burials were interred with a range of ceramic vessels, the forms of which parallel those found in Shanbei culture sites to the east. These third-millennium B.C. sites are found in the Poyang Lake area, and form an important nodal point between the settlements of the Yangzi Valley and those such as Shixia, which probably represent an expansion of settlement to the south.

The lower Yangzi area is also studded with prehistoric mounds that evidence the establishment of rice cultivation. During the period of high sea level, Lake Taihu was a shallow arm of the sea, and its margins would have been a particularly rich habitat. In his analysis of the prehistoric environment of this area, Wu has reconstructed five successive climatic phases on the basis of the changing pollen frequencies and the variations in tropical elements in the fauna from archaeological sites. The climatic change of most interest to us was the marked amelioration which took place between 6000–5000 B.C., when it became warmer again, with a subtropical and humid regime favoring a mixed evergreen and deciduous forest. Elephant, rhinoceros, and alligator remains confirm subtropical conditions (Wu 1983). Wu has also shown that the substratum on the southern margins of the Hangzhou River, just south of the Yangzi delta, comprise lignite. This indicates a low-lying, swampy habitat with numerous lakes. It is evident that the coast was considerably further inland than it is at present, for oyster shell banks have been found under Hangzhou City, but that since 5000 B.C. there has been rapid sedimentation (Zhao and Wu 1988). This led to the formation of many coastal lagoons and marshes, and it was in such a habitat that Hemudu, one of the best-documented early agricultural sites in Southeast Asia, was located.

Hemudu was occupied between 5000–3900 B.C. Huge quantities of rice were found there, including husks, grains, stalks and leaves. This has been identified as a cultivated variety, but the diet was enriched with carp, mullet, and domestic pig. There are many related sites in this low-lying region. Luajiajiao, for example, is located on the southeastern margins of the Yangzi delta, about half way between Hangzhou Bay and Lake Taihu. It belongs to the Majiabang culture, and has revealed the remains of houses raised on stilts, rice, domesticated pig, dog and buffalo, and bone spades. It seems to have been occupied at about the same juncture as early Hemudu (Zhao and Wu 1988). Population expansion is again suggested by the number of later sites ascribed to the Songzhe culture. Pile houses, storage pits, and cemeteries are found, along with much rice, domestic pig, dog and water buffalo bones, and agricultural implements. The passage of time also saw increased evidence for social distinction expressed as impressive quantities of grave goods with certain individuals.

Archaeological research in Southeast Asia has now reached a point where it is possible to plot dated sites that include rice remains on a map, and consider whether they may have expanded out from an original center of domestication. At present, the early sites are in the Yangzi Valley, while later ones are found both to the north and south. Thus, as one proceeds in a southerly direction, sites with rice remains are fewer and later. The initial settlement of Shixia in Qujiang Province, for example, has been dated within the third millennium B.C. This site contains the remains of a clearly domesticated rice, agricultural implements, and a communal cemetery. Chang (1986) has suggested that there was a major expansion of agricultural settlement in China from the seventh to the third millennia, with lowland foci extending from Jilin in the north to Guangdong in the south, and west from Shandong to Gansu. He detects sufficient similarities in these regional traditions to link them all in a "Chinese Interaction Sphere," the name stressing the importance of the spread of peoples, ideas, and goods between each region. Unfortunately, Chang ceased consideration of this phenomenon at the political boundaries of the modern Chinese state. Moreover, to apply the term Chinese to all these regions overlooks the historic fact that the peoples of southern China were incorporated into the Chinese Empire forcibly during the late first millennium B.C., and before then were not Chinese in any sense of the word. We find it more logical to consider the area from the Yangzi to the Chao Phraya as one major cultural area unified by the monsoon climate and significance of rice. It is also highly likely, with the progress of research, that the area should also include Burma and parts of eastern India.

The clear question which must, therefore, be asked is whether the evidence for an expansion of the rice agricultural communities originating in the Yangzi Valley might have had an impact in the broad plains of the Red, Mekong, and Chao Phraya rivers. We have already seen how the Red River links the interior of Yunnan with the Gulf of Bac Bo. There can also be no doubt that coastal movement by boat was well established and would have provided links between Vietnam and the settlements along the coast of southern China. During the past two decades, Vietnamese archaeologists have identified and examined a group of mound sites located in the undulating country above the confluence of the Black and Red rivers. These sites cover between 1 and 3 hectares, and are located on raised terrain commanding small stream valleys. One of the most extensive excavations took place at Phung Nguyen, after which the group as a whole has been named. The researchers encountered a sophisticated pottery industry, in which a favored decorative technique involved burnishing the surface of the vessel before firing and incising parallel bands of decoration, each infilled with a pointed implement, perhaps the edge of a shell. Watson (1983) has noted parallels in this technique between Phung Nguyen and western Chinese sites. There was also a vigorous stone-working tradition. Over a thousand stone adzes were found at Phung Nguyen, as well as many chisels and grinding stones and some arrowheads. Over five hundred stone bracelets were also found, most fashioned from nephrite. Few cemeteries have been investigated, but the one at Lung Hoa is particularly interesting. The graves are cut as deep as 3 meters into the ground, and contain stone jewelry, pottery vessels, and polished stone adzes. Of the 52 Phung Nguyen sites to be examined, 41 had no evidence for metal-working. Only in 11 late sites were a few pieces of bronze encountered, but no recognizable bronze artifacts.

In linking components of his Interaction Sphere, Chang stressed broad similarities in the presence of communal cemeteries, pottery styles, and exotic ornaments. It brings us to one of the central issues to be considered in this book. On the one hand, by adopting Chang's approach, a case could be made for including the Phung Nguyen sites into the same overall scheme and seeking the origins in an expansion of people from the Yangzi Valley. This expansion could then have encompassed the other lowland sites in the Mekong and Chao Phraya drainage systems. On the other hand, the Phung Nguyen and other village communities to the south and west could represent the results of one or more local transitions to rice cultivation. These alternatives will be returned to.

In Chinese tradition, the Truong Son Range formed a major barrier to southern expansion. Yet to the west of the mountains on the Khorat Plateau, there are some sites that recall the principal features of the Phung Nguyen culture. As yet, very little is known about this early settlement of the plateau, but at the base of the site of Ban Chiang and in early contexts at Non Nok Tha, there are burials which are probably contemporary with Phung Nguyen sites. At the former, the early pottery vessels were decorated in a manner reminiscent of the Phung Nguyen incised technique. Similar patterns have also been found at a small but undated site of Non Khao Noi. Cemeteries again include inhumation graves with pottery vessels, the bones of domesticated pigs and cattle, stone adzeheads, and stone and shell jewelry. Some of the pottery was tempered with rice chaff, and there was a preference for settlement in the vicinity of streams where the flood regime would probably have been favorable to rice cultivation.

The Bangkok Plain brings us to the doorstep of Khok Phanom Di. Here again, there are some prehistoric settlements that recall the general features of early Ban Chiang and the Phung Nguyen sites. Khok Charoen, for example, has yielded 49 burials (Ho 1984). The richest had no fewer than 19 pottery vessels, stone beads, and ten shell and nine stone bracelets. Much of the shell is of marine origin. In his consideration of the pottery, Watson (1979) has stressed similarities in form with early wares from Non Nok Tha. The Bang site at Ban Kao is another early village and cemetery site, the early phase being dated between the limits of 2500–1500 B.C. Stone adzes, shell, and stone jewelry, and many polished stone adzes add up to a familiar pattern.

On balance, the available evidence for the origin and spread of rice cultivation in Southeast Asia supports the contention that early steps were taken in the valley of the Yangzi. Population expanded and new communities were established. The further one proceeds to the south, the later the establishment of similar villages becomes. Moreover, with time, it seems that status differentials within the communities represented tended to increase. This simple model of population increase driven by the productive new economy and emphasis on sedentism, while sustained by present dating evidence, will have to be considered in the light of linguistic data. Moreover, it would require modification if evidence were found in the southern part of the area, which includes the Bangkok Plain, for rice cultivation earlier than that documented in southern China.

The initial settlement of the Bangkok Plain, Khorat Plateau, and Red River Valley seems to have taken place some time between 3000 and 2000 B.C. It was followed in all three regions by a period of startling technological innovation involving the extraction of copper and tin, and the casting of objects in bronze. Central Thailand is particularly well endowed with mineral resources. There is a concentration of copper ore deposits in the Khao Wong Prachan Valley, and the northern end of the richest concentration of tin known extends into the uplands to the west. Lead is also present in the Tennasserim Mountains. The Khorat Plateau is ringed by rich mineral sources of copper and tin. Not long after the initial settlement of Non Nok Tha and Ban Chiang, some people were buried with bronze artifacts. At least some of these were locally cast. Indeed at Non Nok Tha there is a grave containing not only a bronze socketed axe, but also the bivalve stone molds in which it was cast. At Ban Chiang, a socketed bronze spearhead, bracelets, and an axe have been found in the graves. One of the best sources of information on a cemetery containing bronzes is Ban Na Di, about 20 kilometers to the south of Ban Chiang.

Excavations there in 1981 identified two distinct cemetery areas, in which the graves were clustered beside and over each other. They were contemporaneous with a clay-lined pit furnace that had been charged with charcoal in order to raise the alloy to melting point. The alloy, contained in small ceramic crucibles, was then poured into the stone molds. The occupants of this site between about 1000–500 B.C. participated in an exchange network which brought not only copper and tin, but also marble, slate, pottery vessels, and marine shell bangles. The concentration of such exotic artifacts in the graves of one of the clusters has led to the suggestion that the autonomous, small community in question was divided into differentially ranked social groups.

The quest for more information on this bronze tradition has led Pigott and Natapintu into the surrounding uplands to seek the prehistoric ore sources. Their first success came at Phu Lon, where a copper mine dating from the second millennium B.C. was excavated (Pigott 1985). This mine, impressive as it is, pales before their more recent research in the Bangkok Plain. In the Khao Wong Prachan valley, they have found a concentration of sites in which copper ore was crushed, then smelted and cast into a variety of artifacts as well as ingots (Pigott and Natapintu 1988). Even the graves of the metal workers have been found, deep in the deposits at Non Pa Wai. Here, we find individuals buried with clay molds for casting an axe and a socketed axehead itself. While clay molds were preferred in the Bangkok Plain sites, in the Red River area, and in the Dong Nai Valley east of the Mekong Delta, stone molds like those from the Khorat Plateau were used more often.

Bronze was cast into bracelets, some of which mirror the earlier forms of stone bracelets. Cast into the form of wire, it was used to repair stone bracelets when they fractured. We also find bronze axes, spearheads, arrowheads, and beads. They found their place, along with other exotic or rare objects, in the graves of women, men, and children.The most economical hypothesis on its origins is that the casting technology was locally discovered in the Bangkok Plain about 1500 B.C.

The results of excavations at Khok Phanom Di should have a bearing on a model for the origins of rice cultivation in the Yangzi Valley, followed by its progressive adoption extending in a southerly direction. According to available radiocarbon dates, such an expansion would have occurred between 5000 and 2000 B.C. There is a second hypothesis, involving a local development of rice agriculture in the valleys of the Chao Phraya, Mekong, and Red rivers, and this, too, could be considered by regional research in any of those areas. The following chapters will consider not only this general issue, but also the fortunes of those who lived at this site over the five centuries of its prehistoric occupation.

2

The Excavation

□

I (CH) first visited Khok Phanom Di in February 1980, when Pisit Charoenwongsa asked if I would like to inspect a newly discovered and unusual site. He was then head of the Research Division of the Fine Arts Department, the government agency charged with all archaeological matters in the Kingdom of Thailand. We drove for about an hour in an easterly direction from Bangkok to the provincial center of Chachoengsao, crossed the bridge over the Bang Pakong River and followed the road south to Phanat Nikhom (Fig. 2.1). After about 12 kilometers, we turned left and followed a narrow winding dirt road, past golden rice stubble on each side. As we passed the first bend, I caught my first glimpse of the site. It lay, like a great stranded whale, dominating the surface of the flat floodplain. Pisit explained that, until recently, the site had been regarded as a natural hill, 12 meters high and covering 5 hectares (Fig. 2.2).

We drove up onto the mound, and, no sooner had we left the car, than Jong, later to be our foreman in four excavation seasons in this area, appeared from his house and welcomed us. The center of the mound is flat, but it rises around the edges, in the form of a saucer. Temple buildings dot this high ground, but I was drawn to a bamboo structure with a thatched roof, for it was under this shelter that Damrongkiadt Noksakul had recently finished an excavation.

The excavation area, covering 5 by 3 meters, remained open, and the ladder that gave access to the lower layers was still there. My first emotion was a mixture of awe and excitement. Damrongkiadt had excavated to a depth of nearly 9 meters before reaching the natural substrate. The climb down his rickety bamboo ladder seemed very long. He had left some human burials in place, and one could see them, still covered in a red ochre pigment, through the gloomy depths of the site. Excitement rose too, because I made myself a promise that one day I would come back and work here. However, I was then on my return journey to New Zealand, having just finished a season at Ban Na Di, 500 kilometers to the northeast on the Khorat Plateau. Much research and writing lay ahead before more fieldwork could be contemplated.

We decided to visit Damrongkiadt, a lecturer at the local teachers' training college. As we drove away, we stopped at the road cutting that gave access to

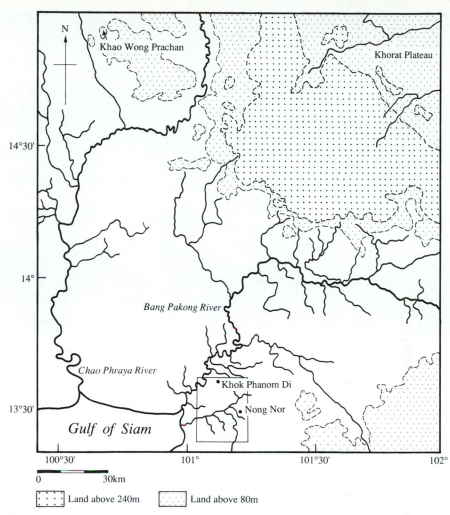

FIGURE 2.1   *Central Thailand, showing the position of Khok Phanom Di within the Bang Pakong Valley archaeological research area.*

the temple buildings. At least 3 meters of prehistoric layers were exposed, lens upon lens of ash, spreads of pottery, and charcoal concentrations. There were shell lenses and thick deposits of pot shards. This exposure had been scraped back and the finds described by the Thai archaeologist Pornchai Suchitta not long after the site had been recognized. He noted that the species of shellfish present are types adapted to a marine habitat, and he radiocarbon-dated a sample of charcoal to about 1500 B.C. If an upper layer was in the second millennium B.C., how old were the deep deposits revealed by Damrongkiadt?

We tracked him down, and he showed us some of his finds. He had encountered 11 burials, the individuals being orientated with their heads towards the rising sun, and often accompanied by complete pottery vessels

FIGURE 2.2   *Khok Phanom Di is the tree-covered mound in the middle distance. It lies like a stranded whale on the floodplain of the Bang Pakong River.*

and shell beads. He showed us a photograph of a cache of rice grains and confirmed the presence of a wide range of remains from marine species. In addition to the shellfish, which were often found in thick layers, there were the remains of crabs, turtles, and many varieties of fish.

My file on Khok Phanom Di was put into a suspense account while my colleagues and I worked on the analysis of the Ban Na Di material. However, I found myself back in Thailand in 1982, and once again visited Khok Phanom Di. Excavations in a rectangular area 7 by 3 meters in extent were in full swing, under the direction of the Thai archaeologist Pirapon Pisnupong. He was down to a depth of about 2.5 meters and was revealing a row of inhumation graves. The dead had been laid out in a line, again with their heads to the east. Burnished black pottery vessels lay beside the skeletons, and some were interred with mushroom-shaped anvils, which had been used to shape clay into pots before firing. The bones were colored red following the ritual spreading of ochre over the bodies. Pirapon also mentioned to me some radiocarbon dates which Damrongkiadt had obtained on the human remains. The lowest burial, found at a depth of 7 meters was dated to 4800 B.C.

This visit was a brief one, for I was on my way to Philadelphia. There, I had the chance to discuss Khok Phanom Di with Rachanie Thosarat. She was completing her master's thesis research before returning to her post with the Fine Arts Department in Bangkok. We had worked together 7 years previously during the excavation of Ban Chiang, near Ban Na Di on the Khorat Plateau. Together, we formulated an ambitious research program not only to excavate Khok Phanom Di, but also to try to illuminate the entire prehistoric sequence in the lower valley of the Bang Pakong River, in which this site lies. The following year, as the publication of Ban Na Di neared, we wrote up our proposal for formal submission to the Thai authorities. Fortune smiled on us, no doubt due to the persistent support for cooperative ventures by Pisit Charoenwongsa, and the permit duly arrived. Now there was one remaining problem, money.

May 1983 saw me once again in Bangkok, and good luck continued: I found myself on the same floor in the same hotel as Tom Kessinger, representative of the Ford Foundation in Southeast Asia. The Foundation had funded a training program for young Thai archaeologists who had worked with me at Ban Na Di, and I nursed an ambition to see it continued at Khok Phanom Di. Over dinner, I came out with a bold question: "How much can I put in for?" His answer was discreet and indirect. "I can't tell you," he said, "how much we budget for any project, but I have the authority to make grants of up to $25,000 without reference to New York." He also confirmed that it would be legitimate to apply for funds for the excavation if it was a focus for training young Thai archaeologists. I returned to New Zealand and prepared two applications, one for the excavation costs, the other to bring four Thai students to take research degrees in my department. Each application, coincidentally, was for fractionally less than $25,000.

But a major excavation was not inexpensive, and I also prepared applications to as many funding agencies as I could think of: the Wenner Gren Foundation in New York, my own university, the British Academy, the Center for Field Research in Boston, and Cambridge University. My reasons for excavating there must have been persuasive, for one by one these institutions wrote offering support. During the course of 1984, I reached a point where I knew I had enough for a small excavation. Only the Ford Foundation, the big one, remained silent.

Let us see what the proposal contained, for it summarizes what we then thought about the impending excavation. In terms of chronology, we were influenced by two factors. The establishment of a coastline during the period of high sea level would have occurred from about 6000 B.C. The dates obtained for basal Khok Phanom Di by Damrongkiadt suggested use of the site by 4800 B.C. Since the burial he had dated was well above the natural substrate, it did not seem unreasonable to suppose that the initial occupation followed soon after the formation of a new shoreline. We already knew of sites in Central and Northeast Thailand dating from the third millennium B.C. which had yielded the remains of rice. In attempting to reconstruct the likely habitat of Khok Phanom Di, therefore, room was found for freshwater swamps behind the mangrove belt, which could have supported wild rice. The absence of any bronze from this site also suggested its abandonment before this alloy became widely available during the second millennium B.C.

Our proposal, therefore, suggested occupation between 6000–2000 B.C. The rich coastal habitat, occupied by a sedentary community which made pottery and consumed food from the shore and river, also harvested rice. Khok Phanom Di, and other as yet undiscovered estuarine sites, could have been centers of population growth that encouraged expansion up the river systems into the drier hinterland. Here, the argument went, rice cultivation in natural swamplands underwrote initial human settlement in the interior of Southeast Asia. My proposal stressed the importance of interdisciplinary research. Cooperation with colleagues skilled in the analysis of pottery, shell, sediments, and rice, to mention but a few specializations, was essential.

I already knew that the occupants of this site made pottery vessels, because of the number of clay anvils, used in shaping clay, which had been found. Brian Vincent, of Otago University, was then working on his doctoral dissertation on the ceramics from Ban Na Di. His geological training had given him the skills necessary to characterize clay on the basis of its constituent minerals and the material used to temper it. He agreed to join us in the field and shoulder the responsibility of analyzing all the clay artifacts. Bernard Maloney, from the Paleoecology Center of the University of Belfast, specializes in the analysis of plant remains, including pollen, from Southeast Asian sites. His agreement to participate guaranteed insight into the ancient environment. Jill Thompson had just completed her postgraduate studies at London University on the analysis of plant remains from archaeological sites, and her experience in flotation, to recover fragile organic material from the excavated material, represented a major step in achieving our objectives. Jacqui Pilditch had worked on the jewelry from Ban Na Di and was to bring her skills in this field to the recovery and analysis of the mortuary ornaments. Numerous other specialists and students were to join the team as research progressed.

But there remained a pressing problem. I still had not heard from Tom Kessinger at the Ford Foundation. It was now August 1984, and excavations were due to start in five months. So I telephoned him. He is very busy, and usually out of the office on his travels. But on this day, I was put straight through and found myself asking if he had decided on my two applications. I heard him ask for the file and then, talking aloud, he went into its contents. "Yes," I heard him say, "they all seem alright. Yes, go ahead, and good luck to you".

He had made up his mind, in the space of 90 seconds, to make everything possible. Perhaps without realizing it, he altered the course of a good many lives. But more immediately, I could now plan in detail. My doctoral student and co-director of the excavation of Ban Na Di, Amphan Kijngam, was still in New Zealand working with me, and we laid an ambitious plan. At Ban Na Di and Ban Chiang, excavations had been laid out in villages where the area was constrained by the presence of houses. In both, the area excavated was long and narrow. In neither was a reasonable area opened to provide information on the spatial dimension of a settlement or cemetery. These sites also tend to be deep, each reaching natural soil about 4 meters below the present surface. One of our laboratories in Dunedin is very large, and has a floor laid out in meter squares to allow finds from a site to be reconstructed under cover. We paced out variously sized excavation areas, and thought of the depth we would encounter. After a number of permutations, we decided simply and boldly to go for a square measuring 10 by 10 meters. Now, we could not contemplate an excavation without a roof. Hitherto, we had used bamboo and thatch, but that would not suffice to cover such an area. Brian Vincent then offered to work with an engineer friend to design a roof of steel. The plans showed 13-meter trusses raised on stout wooden posts, all ringed with a low brick wall. Amphan then took this plan back to Bangkok, leaving with a promise to "arrange everything."

I arrived in Bangkok on December 20, 1984. Rachanie met me with the news that Amphan had finished the roof, and we were all set to start (Fig. 2.3). Our choice of the excavation site had been determined for us. The Abbot of the local Buddhist temple pointed out an area in the central part of the mound. He chose it because it meant that we would not need to damage any of his trees (Fig. 2.4).

Rachanie had gathered a team of colleagues from the Fine Arts Department to help run the excavation. Pirapon Pisnupong was to bring his invaluable experience. Amphan was to work throughout with hardly a day missed. Warrachai Wiriyaromp joined us to help record and draw, and Anat Bamrungwongse was to prove invaluable in every area of the excavation. Phrapid Choosiri was to assist in particular with the treatment of the human remains. Only on reaching the site, however, did I appreciate the magnitude of what lay ahead. A 10 by 10 meter area in our laboratory seemed manageable, but finally on site, it seemed such a huge area that I tried to persuade Amphan to cut it back to 10 by 8. But he stood firm. Anat was already leading cables across to provide light within the square. We had tables prepared for the analysis of shells and pottery, pipes fed water to the washing tables, and another led from the temple's water cistern to the edge of the site where the flotation would take place. There, water would create a head, and once the tap was opened, would bubble up into the base of a large steel tub. Organic

FIGURE 2.3   *The roof covers the area chosen for the excavation of 1984–85. It is in the center of the mound, and was selected by the Abbot of the local temple.*

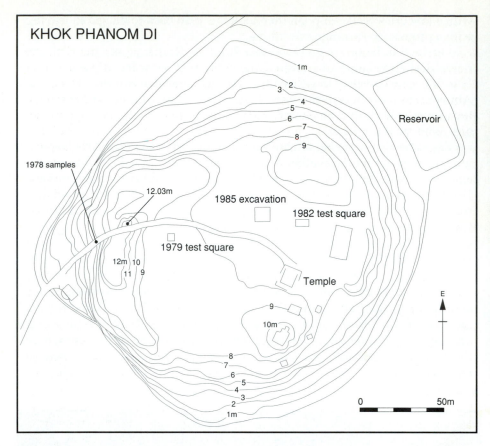

FIGURE 2.4   *Khok Phanom Di is a nearly circular mound, which rises to a maximum of just over 12 meters above the flood plain.*

remains in the excavated soil would then float to the surface, to be trapped in the waiting sieves. A large workforce of local villagers was assembled. We decided to divide the excavated area into four quadrants, and excavate each separately. Because of language problems, each quadrant was given a color code, and all materials coming from a given quadrant had the same color tag as it proceeded from excavation through cleaning and drying to analysis and packaging. On December 27, 1984, excavations commenced.

THE POTTERY WORKSHOP

Layer 1 comprised only recently disturbed material. Layers 2 and 3 contained the latest prehistoric deposits, extending over a depth of about 40 centimeters. The dominating feature was a dump of unfired clay spread over an area of 3 by 1.6 meters. Around it lay many clay anvils and cylindrical lumps of clay. The latter may well have been the first stage in making a vessel: shaping a cylinder later to be formed with the anvil and a paddle. Ninety-five such anvils were found. There were also 22 white pebbles. At first we did not appreciate what these were for, but later analyses showed that they were used to polish, or burnish the surface of a vessel before firing. If this was the place where pots were fashioned, firing must have taken place elsewhere, because hardly any charcoal and no ash deposits were encountered. The surface of the mound, however, is saucer-shaped with a clear rise all round the exterior. The road cutting section revealed many ash lenses and pottery dumps, and it seems probable that, as is still the practice today, pots were taken to the edge of the settlement for firing to avoid the risk of a conflagration. Many other artifacts were found in this late context. There were about sixty broken stone bracelets, several bracelets of turtleshell, ivory, and bone, worked antler, and awls used, we think, in weaving. Perhaps other manufacturing was undertaken in addition to pottery-making, for on the surface of Layer 4 we found a cache of unworked ivory, a complete antler, and the carapace of a turtle. No marine remains were found, the animal bones coming from land species.

WE ENCOUNTER THE CEMETERY

The antler, ivory, and turtleshell lay above a clear break in the stratigraphic sequence. The deposits lightened in color and became more sandy. Numerous pits had been cut from within Layer 4. They contained the remains of shellfish, crabs, fish, and animal bones, showing that access to marine resources was possible. In some parts of the site, there were so many of these pits that they intercut each other. Towards the base of this layer, at a depth of 1.3 meters, we detected a most unexpected feature within the sandy deposit. As we cleaned the surface of the newly exposed surface, we saw a straight line of clay about 15 centimeters wide. It was oriented a few degrees to the north of east, on just the same line as the graves which Pirapon had found. Previously, any prehistoric buildings found in Thailand had been represented by postmolds, circular holes representing the position of wooden posts which in time had rotted, but still left their shadow in the cultural deposits. We were taken aback by this line of clay, and followed its course with considerable interest. It continued on its way for another two meters, and then turned at a right angle to the south. At its other end, it likewise turned a right angle. There, we lost it; someone had dug a pit through it in prehistory, but beyond the pit we recovered its course, and it finally resolved into a rectangular building (Fig. 2.5).

We then began to uncover the surface within the walls of what came during excavations to be known as "the platform." There was clearly a flat surface, like a floor, although it had been punctured by the base of some of the pits which we had found earlier. Along the line of the clay wall, we found lines of postmolds, suggesting a wooden superstructure. Away from this structure, we were also conscious of a marked change in the nature of the deposits, for there were a number of ashy hearths and lenses of reddish soil flecked with charcoal. It was at this juncture that the first human remains were encountered. In the southeast corner, the tibia of a child lay on the same axis as the walls of the building. The remaining tibia and foot bones were found, but the femur lay outside the excavated area. Two pottery vessels had

FIGURE 2.5   *The outline of a raised structure with clay walls is seen. Later excavations revealed that it was a mortuary building raised over the burial of a woman.*

been placed beside the left leg, and a burnishing stone was found beside the right ankle.

The pace of the excavation now perceptibly changed. Fortunately, we had been joined by Damrongkiadt and a team of his students. He proved a superb field illustrator, and before long, he did little other than draw burials. To the west of the platform, the silhouettes of what looked like a row of graves appeared. When a person was buried, the material removed was used to backfill the grave. This was recognizable as a marbled, disturbed deposit, and it revealed the minimum depth at which the grave was cut. As we proceeded through Layers 5 and 6, a row of graves became apparent, at about the same depth and alignment as those found nearby by Pirapon (Fig. 2.6). We also identified numerous postmolds, and followed the course of several ash spreads.

The smallest presumed grave was only 75 centimeters long. We removed 40 centimeters of loose fill before reaching human remains. These came from an infant aged about 9 months at death, with a broken pottery vessel over the ankles. We then followed the line in front of us. A shallow grave next to the woman was found to contain the remains of newly born twins. Next came a grave containing the remains of a woman who died in her mid-twenties. She had been buried with a potter's anvil and two burnishing stones, all between the knee and ankle. Then there was the grave of a male, aged only about 15 years at death. His knees were raised, for there was only just room in the grave to take his body. Two pottery vessels lay beside his right knee. Another infant was found next, this one surviving to about 21 months. A whole pot,

FIGURE 2.6   *The row of burials in front of the raised structure probably contains the remains of three generations of the same family. Their graves were covered by a structure constructed of wooden posts.*

decorated with incised lines, was found at the right shoulder. This infant was also buried with jewelry: four bangles fashioned from the vertebrae of a large fish were found in the area of the right wrist, and nine shell beads were found in the neck area. The seventh grave in this row also contained a more varied set of grave goods. The adult male, who died when about 30 years of age, was found with two pottery vessels, each having broad, flaring rims and round bases. A burnishing stone lay at the right knee and two pieces of worked turtle plastron (the underside) and the carapace (the upper part) of turtleshell were present in the same area. Finally, there was the grave of a second woman who reached her mid-thirties. Two round-based pots were found beside the right knee and left ankle, a third vessel being placed over the left knee. No fewer than eight burnishing stones were found beside the knees.

Beyond the row of postmolds that circled these graves, we identified two discrete ash spreads. During the excavation, there was little time to reflect on the implications of what we were finding. There was too much to do, recording and maintaining momentum. We measured the distance from each artifact found to the fixed points at each corner of the square and fed the distances into a computer to fix the coordinates and depth below the fixed datum point. But as we worked on this row of graves, we could look up at the platform and speculate on the emerging spatial layout of the cemetery.

The stratigraphy on the platform was becoming very complex, for it was made up of successive, thin layers of horizontal fill. We decided to section across its western edge to find out more of its structure, and counted 27 successive such layers, which would have raised the building 50 centimeters above the surrounding surface. It was also at this point that we made out the faint outline of a possible grave in its center. Could this structure have marked a burial? Deep below the clay walls, we found the skeleton of a woman who died in her mid-twenties. She lay on her back on the same orientation as the building above. As we were uncovering her bones, we were conscious of sheets of white fibers. Under our field lens, these turned out to be unwoven fabric: the remains of a shroud. Many more burials were to yield this same substance, some being a beaten bark fabric, others sheets of asbestos. Four pottery vessels had been placed beside the ankles and knees. An anvil and two burnishing stones were found beside the left knee, but the woman's jewelry was considerable: a shell bracelet and 1600 shell beads in the form of thin discs, which also formed bracelets, one round each wrist (Fig. 2.7). The number of beads on this one individual should be compared with the recovery of 12,238 from the entire sample of sixty burials from the first mortuary phase at Ban Na Di.

But this grave, burial 19, was not the only one associated with this structure, for two more individuals had been buried slightly later and to the left of this primary interment. Unfortunately, a prehistoric pit had cut through and removed the legs of both, but even so, their grave goods were impressive. A 42-year-old woman was accompanied by almost 10,000 shell disc beads, and a further seven hundred H-shaped beads. A child, which lay on top of the woman, had 17,186 disc and 656 H-shaped beads, a burnishing stone and a large shell disc beyond the head. Our resolve to open an extensive area had paid a dividend, in the form of the spatial layout of two groups of graves dating to the same period, one rich and enclosed within a raised mortuary building, the other poor and laid out in front of it.

THE PRINCESS

By now, we were into March, and the weather was becoming palpably hotter with each passing day. Brian Vincent was sorting and recording the pottery adjacent to the square, and the mound of analyzed shards was visibly growing. Racks of biological finds from Jill Thompson's flotation work dried in the sun. She was finding charred seeds, fragments of rice, and, most unexpectedly, tiny snails. Bernard Maloney had almost completed his coring around the site. He brought back from the field segments of the deposits seven meters thick which predated the prehistoric occupation. The excavation was now down to a depth of 2.5 meters, and a bamboo ladder was necessary. The mortuary structure had been removed, and we continued down

FIGURE 2.7   *The primary interment under the raised structure contained a woman buried with whole pots, a shell bracelet, burnishing stones, a clay anvil, four pottery vessels, and over one thousand shell beads. She died in her mid-twenties.*

into Layer 7, which was distinctive for its ashy lenses and concentrations of shellfish. Many postmolds were recognized, but relatively few artifacts. Only three clay anvils were found in all of Layer 7, a handful of burnishing stones, and a single stone adzehead. There were also some bangles of stone, ivory, and turtle shell, and some bivalve shells which had clearly been modified, for their outer surfaces were worn to a concave cutting edge.

We made a point of regularly scraping the surface of the excavated area clean as we proceeded down, for changes in soil color or texture were of the greatest significance in our quest for pattern and structure. As we were cleaning in our southwestern quadrant, we detected a straight line. On one side, there was undisturbed white ash, on the other, the mixed fill that heralded a grave. The line continued for a good 2 meters. It should, in theory, have turned a right angle at the head of the grave, but it steadfastly continued, like a Roman road. Another meter, and finally it turned to the north. It was the outline of a very large feature indeed, three meters long, a meter wide. Burial 4, at a higher level, had just impinged onto its northwestern edge. We began to remove the marbled fill with an air of considerable expectation, whetted when we encountered the rim of a complete pottery vessel only a few centimeters down. Then there was a second rim; this could only be a very large grave. At this point, we found that the pots had been placed upon a pyramid of clay cylinders that we had already interpreted as representing an early stage in the manufacture of pots.

The human remains came unexpectedly. At a depth of 80 centimeters, we came across a deep red stain: it was the skull of someone who had been buried under a profusion of red ochre. We followed the path of the skeleton and marveled at the richness of the grave goods: two shell discs at each side of the skull, and over the shoulders, circular shell discs with horns emerging from the center (Fig. 2.8). We had never seen such artifacts in prehistoric Southeast Asia before. On the chest there were row upon row of shell disc beads mingled with large, translucent I-shaped beads. A heavy shell bracelet was found on the left wrist, and superb black and richly ornamented pottery

FIGURE 2.8   *Burial 15, known as "The Princess," was accompanied by much shell jewelry, broken pottery vessels, and the tools for making pots. The body was covered by cylinders of clay thought to have been stored for later shaping into ceramic vessels.*

vessels lay over the legs. A large bivalve shell containing two burnishing pebbles lay upturned beside the right ankle. Alongside was the clay anvil to complete the potter's tool kit. The pelvis indicated the remains of a woman. It was many months before we were able to count the shell disc beads, for when we finally removed her from the ground, an equal number were found under her back. She had clearly worn a garment encrusted with rows of brilliant reflective shells (Fig. 2.9). Someone christened her "the Princess of Khok Phanom Di." The final count was 120,787 disc and 950 large I-shaped beads. We made an obeisance to the Abbot for so wisely determining where we should dig, and he acknowledged us inscrutably.

Two meters to the north, we came across another straight line cut through a lens of ash. This one was not so long, but it was parallel with the Princess's grave. We began removing the fill and again came across the splash of red ochre over the skull. This grave, easily large enough for an adult, contained the skeleton of an infant aged about 15 months at death (Fig. 2.10). There was a pile of clay cylinders over the body, and a profusion of shell disc beads. Two

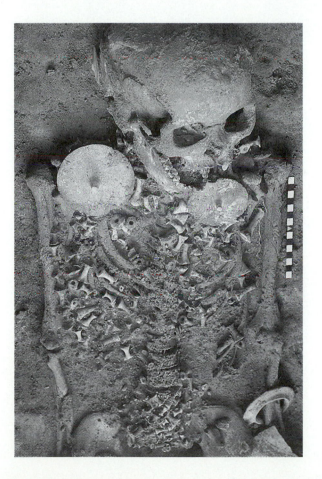

FIGURE 2.9   *The shell jewelry from burial 15 included over 121,000 beads, discs, a bracelet, and components of what was probably a headdress.*

hundred I-shaped and 12,247 disc beads lay over and behind the chest. Some formed a bracelet, others a belt. A shell bangle lay over the left wrist, and four black burnished pottery vessels were present over the legs. To complete the pattern, we found a burnishing stone and a miniature clay anvil next to the right ankle. This tiny anvil, little more than a toy, was to exercise us greatly when we were to try to interpret the significance of these finds.

But there was more to come. Beyond the feet of the Princess's grave and to the south, we encountered yet another grave, this time circular. Within it lay two large pottery vessels facing each other, one of which was the largest found at the site. These enclosed the skeleton of another 15-month-old, with two smaller vessels at the feet and 269 shell disc beads. At the eastern edge of the square there was yet another grave of considerable wealth. A man in his early thirties had been buried with a huge shell bracelet, a turtle carapace ornament, two shell discs, 435 I-shaped, and 56,200 shell disc beads. As we edged slightly deeper in the vicinity of the Princess, our burial 15, there was yet another grave. This one was so narrow that there was barely room

FIGURE 2.10   *The infant interred alongside burial 15 was treated in a virtually identical way, even down to the provision of a tiny anvil next to the right ankle.*

for the corpse. In it, we found the remains of a young man aged about 21. The grave was hard up against burial 15, and the man was headless. His grave goods amounted to two simple pots.

THE FIRST EVIDENCE FOR CLUSTERS OF BURIALS

We were now down to a depth of three meters. To judge from Pirapon's nearby square, we had another five meters to go. April now beckoned, the hottest month preceding the rains of May. We thought in terms of reaching four meters, halfway down, and then closing the excavation until the following dry season. As we excavated into Layer 8, we continued to find anvils, burnishing stones, numerous shell knives, and, for the first time, a bone fishhook. Pierced clay netweights also provided evidence for fishing. There was also a new series of graves, which again contrasted with those we had already encountered. The dead were usually interred in an individual grave, but on several occasions, there were double inhumations. Burials 21 and 23, for example, were interred in the same grave, a 30-year-old man and a child of about 8. The former was accompanied by a burnishing stone and a turtle carapace ornament; the latter had nothing. Burial 31 was likewise interred in the same grave as 32, one a woman aged about 25, the other an 11-year-old. The child was accompanied by a pottery vessel and a carved turtle carapace ornament with a hole in the middle, while the woman had a complete pot by the ankles. In the northern corner of the square, 10 graves were found beside and over one another in a concentrated group. There were men, women, children, and infants. Grave goods included pottery vessels, anvils, burnishing stones, and turtle carapace ornaments. Most pottery vessels had the form of carinated, round-bottomed bowls with flaring rims, lacking the size and decoration of their successors.

Another concentration of similar interments was found in the eastern part of the square. Again, the grave goods were few and simple. Hardly any shell disc beads, or indeed shell jewelry of any sort, was found. One woman, who died when in her early to mid-twenties, held a new-born infant in her left arm (Fig. 2.11). Two other women, burials 35 and 36, were interred in a linear arrangement, where the raised structure would one day be built. Field impressions are very unreliable, but there could be little doubt that these people were buried with far less ritual and conspicuous display of jewelry than their successors.

Songkhran is the name given to a day towards the end of April when the temperature reaches its zenith. A leaden sun scorches down; the storm clouds heralding the rains are near. It is a day when everyone lets their hair down, and splash water over each other. We arrived at the excavation to be greeted with buckets of water, and damp clothes were the order of the day. We also edged past a depth of four meters. At this point in his sequence, Pirapon had passed through the cemetery phase and was to find no more burials, only layer upon layer of ash and shell midden. When we began, we estimated on the basis of his finds that we would find about forty burials. We had achieved this. Now should we close down ahead of the rains?

FIGURE 2.11   *Burials 47 and 48: A woman who died in her early twenties, with a newly born infant on her left shoulder.*

We discussed alternatives with Amphan. Already plants were beginning to grow out of the upper walls of the square and had to be trimmed. Several months delay would inevitably lead to the walls' eroding and beginning to cave in. What if the rains and flooding invaded our defensive wall and filled the square? Realistically our only option was to continue, but only if further funds could be found. Time was of the essence, but fortune smiled. A few weeks previously, Tom Kessinger had visited us with Dr. Botero, one of the trustees of the Ford Foundation. Tom seemed impressed with our progress. We approached him for a supplementary grant, and after a few days of anxiety, the message came back from Jakarta: the check was in the mail.

By now, Damrongkiadt and his team of students had departed. Brian Vincent and Bernard Maloney had left for home. Jill Thompson remained at the flotation tank, only now it would prove increasingly difficult to dry samples due to the onset of the rains. Excavating was much more demanding. Rain came in occasional, violent storms. We had already built a deep drain to take water off the center of the mound, which would otherwise have been quickly transformed into a lake. Every few paces, there were brick-lined sediment traps that had to be cleaned out after every downpour. Sometimes the drain simply overflowed, and we had to build sandbag walls to prevent water from filling the square. On more than one occasion, water would find a weak point and simply cascade into the excavation from the wall of the square, threatening a major slump. But with our local labor force, we carried on down. Our prediction that we had reached the earliest graves was confirmed, for Layer 9 turned out to comprise a series of solid midden lenses, much evidence of burning activity, and many pits and postmolds. Shell knives were particularly abundant, with a total of 47, and there were 33 burnishing stones.

On one occasion in mid-May, we had to attend a meeting in Bangkok. It was late afternoon when we returned to Khok Phanom Di. We glanced down into the square, and there, now deep below us, were more graves. And they directly underlay the concentrated groups that we had found a fortnight previously. We noticed, over the next period of the excavation, a number of changes as well. There seemed to be many more infant graves. Burial 57, for example, contained a man in his mid-twenties. A turtle carapace ornament had been placed to the right of his chest and two pottery vessels lay beside the shoulder and the feet respectively. He also had a necklace of shell disc beads. Alongside him were the graves of four newly born infants, each in a separate grave, but none with any grave offerings. The man was buried directly over the grave of a woman who was in her late forties, very old by the standards of the day. She had no grave goods, and nearby were the graves of six newly born infants.

Two meters to the north lay another set of graves: three women, all with one or two pots, and three infants. These lay over a 40-year-old man with two newly born infants. He was accompanied by three pots. The pattern was repeated to the east, with a concentration of 16 graves. The richest of these was that of a man in his early thirties. His grave goods suggest that he was rather a singular individual. Apart from three richly ornamented pots, he also had 330 disc beads, three burnishing stones, and some most unusual items, including a worked shell of the species *Nautilus pompilius.* This is a deep-sea shellfish, and it was probably borne to the area of Khok Phanom Di by ocean currents. He also had a worked shark dorsal fin spine (Fig. 2.12). Beyond his head was a grave just large enough to house two newly born infants, each covered in red ochre, and with the heads pointing to the east.

It was while working on these remains that one of our Thai colleagues, Metha Wichakana, made a most unusual discovery. As he was exposing the pelvic area of burial 56, a woman who died in her mid-forties, he encountered a mass of tiny bones. At first, we thought it was a fetus, and that the woman had died in childbirth. But the bones were far too small, and turned out to be from fish, interspersed with fish scales. We had found food remains, possibly representing this person's last meal. Another grave contained some human excrement. Both were to attract much attention in the laboratory.

Two new features were also identified at this stage of the excavation. The groups of burials were surrounded by a deep shell midden with a remarkable characteristic. Although up to a meter deep, it followed straight lines and turned corners. A shell dump, of course, spreads out at its edges. This

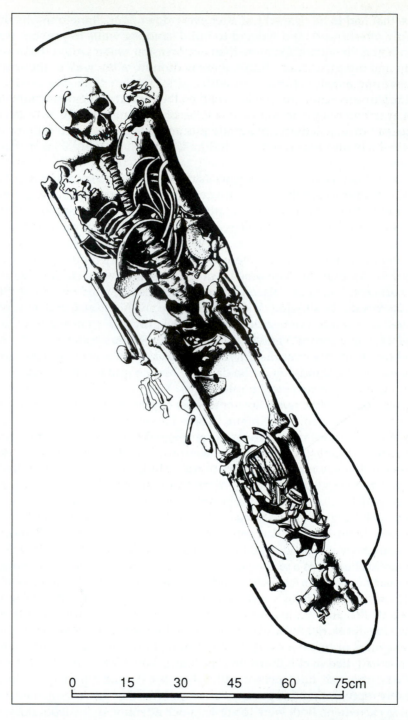

FIGURE 2.12   *Burial 72 contained the remains of a man who died during his early thirties. He was buried with some unusual items: a Nautilus shell, a pendant made from the fin spine of a shark, and a pig's canine tooth. A fish skeleton had been placed at his left shoulder.*

one did not, and the only reasonable explanation seems to be that the shells were deposited against a barrier, such as a wall. Secondly, the groups of graves were associated with pits. These were cut rather carefully, to a circular shape, and they contained the remains of food. Many of the shells in them were unopened.

We had now reached a depth of over 5 meters, and the cemetery showed no sign of terminating. The high number of infants continued; the same particular areas were still used for burials. A male and a female, both in their thirties, were found with four newly born infants and a 4-year-old child. The woman had five burnishing stones and a pottery vessel, the man 220 shell disc beads. His grave had also been laid out with the head pointing to the northeast, so that it just fit between the graves of the three infants and that of the adjacent woman. A further pattern now appeared. People were buried successively from north to south. In most cases, infants were the first to be interred, to be followed by adults. Burials 138 and 127, for example, were infants buried in sequence from the north. There followed burial 115, a male in his late thirties, with another infant at his left shoulder. Burial 87, a woman in her mid-twenties, came last. There were many more grave goods than we had become used to. Burial 132, a man, was interred with 39,000 shell disc beads and 11 of a variety only encountered in the lower graves, shaped like a barrel. The pottery vessels also took on new forms, and more elaborate incised designs. Yet we found no more turtle carapace ornaments with the men. Some children, too, were well endowed with offerings. Burial 133 was an infant who died when about 4 months old. It was accompanied by seven bangles fashioned from the vertebrae of a large fish, 45 barrel beads, six cylindrical shell beads and 17 cowrie shells. Burial 123, a two-year-old, had three elaborately ornamented pottery vessels, a burnishing stone, and 120 shell disc beads. At this juncture, we also found that some of the dead had been placed on wooden biers, for the wood survived under the skeletons.

Away from the graves, many artifacts were turning up. Anvils, fishhooks, burnishing stones, stone hoes, shell knives, and netweights were still found. There were also numerous shell middens, containing thousands of individual shells. We were unsure why these shell middens should be found in such close conjunction with the burial areas, but later consideration of their relative distribution suggested that they may represent mortuary feasting.

At a depth of 5.60 meters, the burials at last began to diminish. Our thoughts turned increasingly to finishing. We checked the depth against that recorded by Pirapon. It seemed as if there was at least another 2 meters to go. Life after Khok Phanom Di was keenly anticipated: the prospect of not getting up early, working away all day down in the depths, and arriving home exhausted at sunset. One final heave, we thought, and it will be over.

But as we left the burials above us, we encountered a whole new dimension. There were thick but discrete shell middens, all of which had to receive special treatment. We now began to find white ash lenses and hearths, sometimes singly, occasionally in rows. There were rows of postmolds, some of which actually still contained the original wood in place. The deposits were rich in organic remains, including fragile leaves, nuts, fragments of rice husk, and fish scales. We seemed to have found deposits where people lived, shaped and fired their pots, and cooked their food.

Nor were the burials completely a thing of the past. As we passed the 6-meter mark, we came across yet more. Again, they had their heads pointing to the east. One contained a handful of shell beads; a child was interred in a shell midden, crouched in a fetal position.

At 6.5 meters, we dug a small hole in the southwestern corner, praying to encounter the natural substrate. But the deposits continued on down. We took charcoal samples from the numerous hearths for radiocarbon dating and found where the inhabitants had placed a cache of adzes, a clay anvil, and some burnishing stones in the ground, never to retrieve them. Thick ash spreads indicated where people had probably fired their pots, and some shards were found to be encrusted with barnacles—the site must have been very low-lying and overrun by seawater. Then, at last, we saw the promised land, the sandy natural substrate. We stood 7 meters below the datum we had set in place last December. It was July 17, 1985.

3

The Analysis

◘

The months following the excavation provided an opportunity for reflection. We had recovered 154 burials, tons of pottery, well over a million shellfish, approximately 250,000 shell beads, and numerous other artifacts. There were animal bones, sediment cores, charcoal, seeds, and the radiocarbon samples. Permission to ship this material to New Zealand had to be obtained, and a timetable for analysis established. The second part of the Ford Foundation support involved Thai students' coming to New Zealand for postgraduate study. We closed down the excavation anticipating confirmation of initial settlement in the sixth millennium B.C., but had only the vaguest impressions of the social organization, subsistence, and technological aspects of the extinct community which we had encountered. Many years of laboratory work lay ahead.

By the end of 1985, a container of finds was on the high seas, heading for Dunedin, and permission had been given in Bangkok for four Thai officials of the Fine Arts Department to take leave in order to study the material. Rachanie Thosarat enrolled for a Ph.D., her topic being the social organization at Khok Phanom Di, based on the mortuary remains. Pirapon Pisnupong and Phrapid Choosiri came as M.A. students. The former expressed an interest in looking at the stone artifacts; the latter wished to study the human remains. Amphan Kijngam took charge of the analysis of fish, turtles, and crabs.

THE CHRONOLOGY

In a preliminary report on our finds, which relied on little more than field impressions, we suggested a chronological framework based on the results that had been obtained by Damrongkiadt. Dates had been processed in Bangkok on the basis of human bone samples. Fortunately, we had an abundance of charcoal to date from discrete lenses and hearths. We chose six, representing Layers 8 and 9, and submitted them to the laboratory of the Department of Scientific and Industrial Research (D.S.I.R.) in Wellington, New Zealand. The lowest of the samples was still 2.5 meters from the bottom of the site. It was dated to 4410 plus or minus 300 B.C. Such radiocarbon dates have to be corrected for the secular effect to obtain the actual estimate B.C. When this was done, we found that there is a 95 percent chance of the actual date's falling between 3685–2275 B.C. So far, so good. In order of antiquity, the other five dates came out as follows: Layer 9:6, 2390–1780 B.C.; Layer 9:1, 1812–1310 B.C.; Layer 8:7, 1925–1225 B.C.; Layer 8:3, 2565–1895 B.C. and Layer 8:2, 590 B.C.–A.D. 665. We were disappointed by this group of dates. They did not form a pattern. The last was clearly far too late; it was not possible to present a coherent picture.

At this juncture the Government of New Zealand required the laboratory at the D.S.I.R. to impose full cost charges for its dating facility. We had no funds for this new expense and had to defer further consideration of the site's chronology. In the interim, however, we had to consider the fate of all the organic material that Jill Thompson had recovered through flotation. Only one institution could provide the necessary supervision and the funds: The Australian National University. Douglas Yen, one of the world's leading specialists on the analysis of prehistoric rice remains, was on the staff, and they offered scholarships for doctoral studies. Fortunately for our project, Jack Golson, head of the Department of Prehistory, backed Jill's application, and she was admitted. This vital decision not only guaranteed the analysis of the plant remains so carefully gathered, but also meant that we could date more charcoal samples at the Australian National University free of charge.

Twelve samples were dispatched, and the long wait was borne as patiently as possible. So much hinges on bolting down a site's chronology. A set of contradictory dates, as has afflicted a number of sites in Southeast Asia, helps nobody. The most important point is that the dates be internally consistent. Having early dates at the end of a sequence and later ones at the beginning is an archaeologist's nightmare, particularly in cases like Khok Phanom Di, where there are no similar sites, already dated, in the vicinity.

We learned more about Khok Phanom Di on the day the results arrived than on any other occasion. The result sheets for each date contain a mass of figures, and it takes an hour or two to find out whether or not there is a reasonable pattern. At first, I felt that we had a serious problem on our hands: the dates all seemed far too late. But by degrees, a pattern emerged, rather like seeing an image appear in the photographic darkroom. The first set to become available came from the D.S.I.R. in Wellington. It seemed to support a long period of occupation. The second set from Australia is internally consistent, and suggests a shorter span, perhaps little longer than four or five centuries.

The dates reveal a site that was occupied for a far briefer time than we had imagined. It also was initially settled about four thousand years later than our original estimate. The uppermost layers did not contain sufficient charcoal for dating, so the latest context dated was in Layer 6 (1930–1310 B.C.). The lowest context, a hearth very near the base of the mound, was 2130–1700 B.C. What impressed us was the consistency of the series, which indicated a site with an occupation span of a few centuries, certainly not thousands of years. We concluded that settlement for five hundred years from about 2000 B.C. was the most reasonable interpretation of the Australian radiocarbon series.

THE BURIALS: THE CLUSTERS DEFINED

This conclusion had an immediate bearing on the nature of the mortuary sequence. A build-up of 6 meters of deposit in thousands of years would imply that burial activity was intermittent, with long periods of inactivity. A timespan of centuries would be compatible with an unbroken mortuary tradition. We sat round a table, with all our burial plans in front of us, to try to make some sense of what we had found. We began with the Princess, burial 15. This interment provided what seemed a useful benchmark, for only four burials were found to have been contemporary with her, and their treatment differed from what had happened before. Setting aside all the later material, we concentrated first on the distribution of graves within the excavated area. It seemed as if there was a pattern: groups of graves were clustered, with spaces in between them. So we did two things. First, we drew up a plan, placing on it an outline of all the graves. This confirmed our impressions. Then Glen Standring, a student who had worked on the excavation to the bitter end, volunteered to undertake a statistical analysis of the distribution, using computer graphics to plot the concentrations of graves in three dimensions. Again, discrete rises and falls showed a pattern of groups.

The location of each grave was then considered, and we assigned it, if possible, to one of a number of groups which we named clusters, beginning with cluster A and finishing with I. The location of each cluster showed remarkable consistency, so we then considered them in relation to other features which we had identified. During MP2 (mortuary phase 2), for example, we found that burials in each cluster were interred sequentially in a north–south direction, and were accompanied by oval or circular pits that contained food remains (Fig. 3.1). There were also numerous postmolds. During MP3, a thick shell midden skirted the clusters, and on at least one occasion in the section through the deposits, we found the midden abutting a postmold (Fig. 3.2). Wooden posts have a short life in the tropics, decay and insects taking their toll in a few years. Such posts, therefore, have to be constantly replaced, and the palimpsest of postmolds did not present an easily recognized pattern. Nevertheless, some alignments seemed to follow the same orientation of the graves, suggesting the existence of wooden collective burial structures. As we proceeded higher, to consider some of the later graves, we found that shell middens became fewer and thinner, but discrete ash spreads lapped up to and around graves, as if burning the ground had preceded burial.

Slowly, it was beginning to dawn on us that we might have stumbled on a unique body of prehistoric evidence. Could these graves, located in such a pattern alongside and over each other, be the remains of successive members of the same family through many generations? This caused us to pause and reflect. Cemeteries are a major source of information on prehistoric societies, but normally they are not of long duration, or they are extensive. People were buried alongside each other but the accumulation of archaeological deposits is usually slow, so that successive generations are not buried over each other in an orderly sequence. At Khok Phanom Di, however, the accumulation of deposits was very rapid. A shell midden, for example, or an ash deposit, can

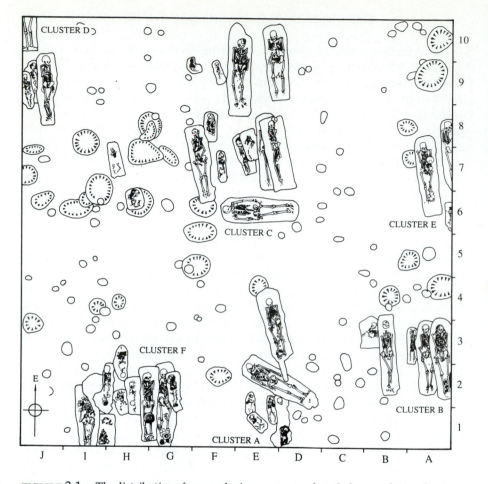

FIGURE 3.1   *The distribution of graves during mortuary phase 2 shows a clustered pattern. The larger circles are pits; the smaller are postmolds which might represent wooden structures around the clusters of graves. Scale in meters.*

reach a considerable thickness in hours. On average, the site accumulated at a rate of about 30 centimeters during a 25-year generation. Moreover, at Khok Phanom Di the many lenses and clear grave cuts, as well as the impinging of one grave cut into that of its neighbor, made possible a very detailed and accurate burial sequence. If our suspicions were true, then here was a key to unlocking the operating heart of the Khok Phanom Di community, its kinship system.

But much more information was needed before this proposal could be tested. First, we needed the sex and age of each individual. At this stage, the human bones were still being pieced together and prepared for analysis. And who was to undertake the diagnosis of the people's life history, their stature, age at death, health, and nutrition? Phrapid had made a start, but her study for the M.A. degree would not cover all these variables. Our expert in the Medical School, Philip Houghton, was far too busy to do the work

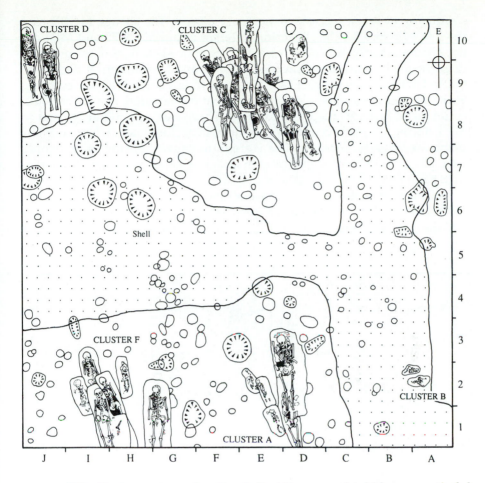

FIGURE 3.2   *During mortuary phase 3, a shell midden accumulated (shown as a stippled area). It skirts the burial clusters and turns right angles. It would hardly have followed this plan had the shells not accumulated against a fence or buildings of some sort. Scale in meters.*

himself. During that year, however, a graduate from Auckland University, Nancy Tayles, had come to Otago to follow up her interest in Southeast Asian prehistory. After a one-year diploma course, she was looking for an interesting topic for her doctoral research. We suggested that the people of Khok Phanom Di would fit the bill and after due consideration, she accepted. Philip Houghton agreed to supervise her work.

As their identifications became available, it became possible to look in more detail at the burial succession in each of the clusters. Before doing so, we found it convenient to identify changes in ritual, of which the change to the rich burial 15 is the most obvious. We began at the beginning, and found that the first six interments, while setting the trend in terms of orientation and basic treatment, were not grouped in any way. The bodies of two men, a woman, and three infants were buried in the occupation deposits with no clear evidence of attendant ritual. We assigned these six burials to the first of a sequence of seven successive mortuary phases. The change to MP2 saw the first evidence for the clustering together of burials. MP2 and MP3 did not differ markedly from each other, but we noticed changes in the quantity of grave goods, particularly the shell jewelry, and two clusters at the southern end of the square (B and E) did not carry through into MP3, unless being at the edge of the square, a slight movement of the burial area to the south could mean that we failed to find them. There was a period at the end of MP3, during which 60 centimeters of deposit accumulated, when no interments were made. When burials were found again, during MP4, people were placed in individual graves with far fewer grave goods, and, in particular, hardly any shell beads (Fig. 3.3).

MP5 is represented by the "Princess" and the other three very rich interments, one of which is not seen in Figure 3.4 because only the ankles extended into the excavated area, while MP6 graves were those found under the raised

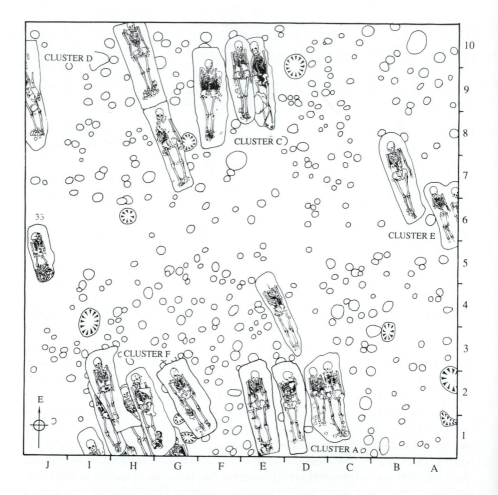

FIGURE 3.3   *The distribution of graves during mortuary phase 4 shows that there were far fewer infants, and that the dead were now buried in individual graves. Scale in meters.*

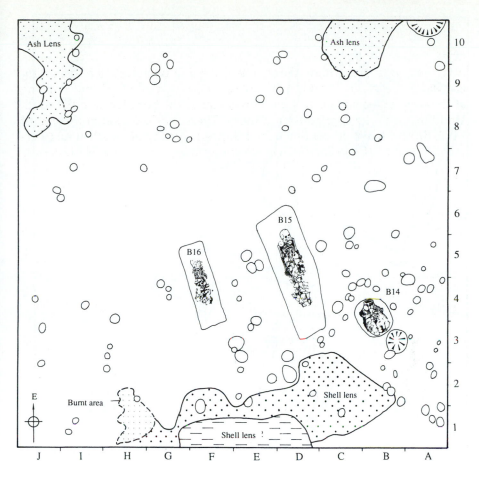

FIGURE 3.4   *The graves belonging to mortuary phase 5 reflect a break in the pattern of clustering individuals. Scale in meters.*

structure and in a row to the front of it (Figs. 3.4–5). The seventh and last mortuary phase comprised four graves, all at the eastern edge of the square.

Having defined these broad chronological divisions, we were in a position to examine the minute details of the burial succession in each of the clusters. By identifying the precise sequence, we hoped to test the hypothesis that, at least in biological terms, these people could have been descended from each other. The earliest MP2 burials in cluster C were a woman aged about 17, and a child of 8. Now, could so young a female have already borne at least one child, leaving another to survive to the next generation? According to Houghton (1975), pregnancy may leave physical modifications to the female pelvis. This scarring cannot be used to identify how many children a woman bore, but it is an indicator of the likelihood that an individual had no children, few, or many. In this case, burial 140 probably had a few. Stage 2 burials in this cluster overlay the earlier two. We have the remains of a woman, a man, and four infants, three of which were newly born, the fourth surviving until about 5 years. This child and one of the infants were found in

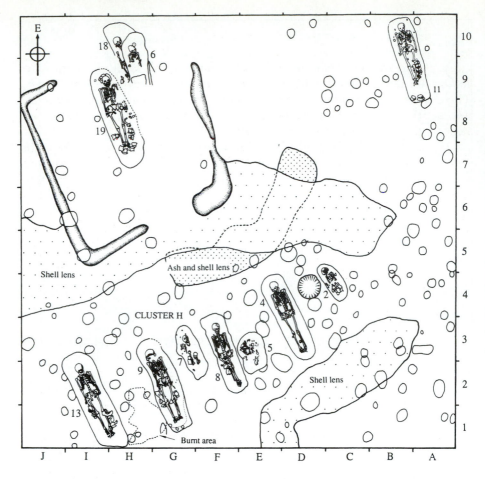

FIGURE 3.5   *With mortuary phase 6, people were again clustered, but either within a mortuary structure or linearly in front of it. Scale in meters.*

the same grave. In the third stage, there was a woman and two infants, and in the fourth, two men, a woman, and a newly born infant. There followed a man and a woman buried beside each other, together with two infants, perhaps twins, found together in the same grave. These were succeeded by a man and a woman buried together, and the remains of a 6-month-old child. Stage 7 saw two females interred in adjacent graves, one with an infant. Stage 8 was represented by a child of 9 and the following Stage 9 by two women, one buried holding an infant in her left arm. Again, two women comprise Stage 10, both aged about 21 years at death. So far, every woman except one revealed the pelvic scarring consistent with pregnancy.

We had reached MP5 when the trail went cold, but the data seemed to support our hypothesis. We therefore turned to cluster F to see if a similar pattern was present. This cluster also began with a woman and child beside each other. Then, in a southerly direction, was another woman with three infants aged between 4 and 18 months at death. There followed a man, with the remains of a 9-month-old over his left side, with four other infant burials in the vicinity. The next stage comprised another male, interred just after two infants of identical size in the same grave. We then come to a woman and two infants, then two more women, one with a newly born infant. Then came a man and a woman, the former sharing a grave with an infant who lay on her left shoulder, with an infant of about 9 months between them. These were overlain by a man and a woman, then another man and woman, and another woman. Fewer infants were encountered at this juncture. The next stage comprises two children of about 12 and a man.

Here, once again, the trail ends with the interment of burial 15. We were reluctant to leave this trail, however. It seemed that where someone was buried mattered greatly, and this should provide some leads. We noted, for example, that the very rich child, burial 16, lay directly beyond the head of burial 8, the youth who had fitted into his grave only when his legs were bent. Burial 15 itself lay below and just beside burial 4, which in turn was directly over burial 22, the headless man. There were some clues, therefore, that the Princess was linked to some later graves, but what of her predecessors? We considered the layout from all angles, and noted that 17, the last so far identified for cluster F, was in a direct line to the headless male and so on to burial 15. So we made an assumption that the Princess was descended from cluster F, and tried to carry on with our family line. The Princess herself was the next female, with her two infants buried in the vicinity. Then we continue with the line of graves in front of the raised structure. First, there was a woman, then an infant and a teenager. An adult man followed, then three infants, and finally, a woman. If the same principles of location are applied to cluster C in its relationship to the raised structure, then there are grounds for linking the two. This cluster indeed would continue with a woman, burial 19, followed by another woman and a child. It is not possible to trace other clusters over such a long sequence. These groups may have died out due to high mortality, or perhaps a group moved to found a new settlement, or even shifted the location of their communal grave to an unexcavated part of the site.

Having proposed that we have at least two successful family groups represented by clusters C and F, it was necessary to find as many ways of testing the hypothesis as possible. The first approach was to set out these family trees, and see if, over the same period of time, there was a similar number of supposed generations. We found that each revealed about 16 (Fig. 3.6). If we ascribe twenty years to each generation, and allow one or two extra for mortuary phases 1 and 7, then four centuries are in question, a comfortably reassuring match with the radiocarbon dating.

We then sought other ways of testing the hypothesis, and four were set in train. Philip Houghton confirmed that some skeletal features, particularly in the skull and dentition, are genetically determined. If one or both parents have a particular characteristic in the skull, such as a wormian bone or an os inca, then their offspring will probably inherit it. Phraphid Choosiri began to pursue this issue as part of her dissertation research.

Having proposed social continuity between these mortuary phases, it is now necessary to consider the likelihood that the superimposition of graves in clusters represents lineages and that individuals are consanguinally or affinally related. In considering this issue, we may begin with Choosiri's analysis

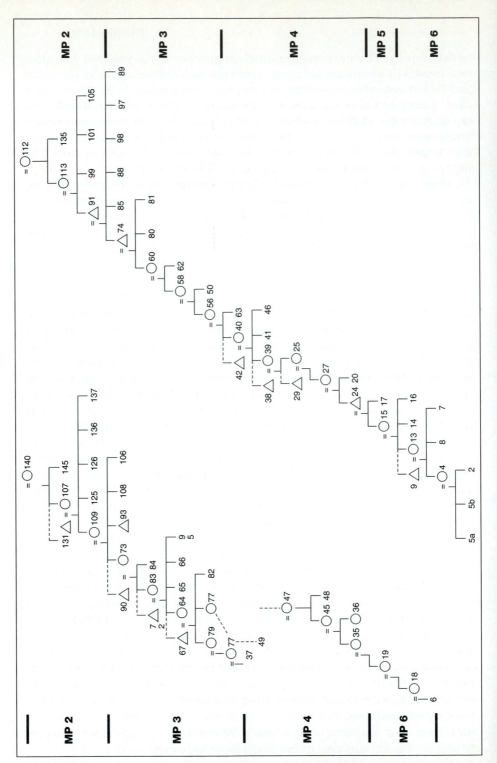

FIGURE 3.6   *The proposed genealogies for clusters C and F. Triangles represent males and circles, females. Other burials are infants or children in which the sex is unknown, and figures refer to the burial number. Dotted lines linking males and females indicate that their relationship is not known.*

of a series of genetically determined features in the crania, teeth, and postcra-
nial bones. These allow the possibility of isolating relationships between individuals through time. It is held that, if such characteristics are present in
individuals interred in the same cluster, then it increases the likelihood that
we are dealing with consanguines. The insight provided by this source of information is first considered on the basis of people buried in the same grave or
in very close physical and chronological relationship. In the case of cluster E
stage 3, we encounter a male and young child in the same grave (Bs. 23 and
21), alongside the grave of a female (B. 26), who had probably borne two or
three children. Whereas the male and female have no such unusual features in
common, the child's cranium combines nearly all those found in the two
adults. The presence of sagittal wormian bones in the crania of burials 21 and
23 is particularly interesting. Only four instances of this feature were present
in the entire sample from the site. It is likely, on the basis of this evidence, that
the three individuals represent a father, mother, and child.

The same situation is found with cluster H. Burials 8 and 9 are a 15-year-
old and an adult male respectively. They were buried beside each other.
They are also the only individuals in the site whose crania have a bregmatic
bone at the intersection of the coronal and sagittal sutures. Burials 9 and 4,
those of an adult male and female, share the retention of the medio-frontal
suture (metopism). The four crania from burials 4, 8, 9, and 13 have lamb-
doid wormian bones and a parietal foramen, while burials 4, 8, and 13 have
a posterior condylar foramen. Such links tend to confirm the hypothesis that
individuals comprising the respective clusters were related to each other.

Given this situation, the successive stages of clusters A, D, C, and F have
been linked in a series of genealogies. It is self evident that this begins from
a speculative position, but it is possible to assess its worth on two counts.
The first is whether the successive "generations" display chains of individuals having the same genetic abnormalities. Secondly, it is suggested that,
if the pattern of tooth evulsion was determined other than in an *ad hoc* manner, successive generations should follow the same or similar pattern of
tooth extraction.

Three conditions in particular show a marked concentration among people belonging to cluster C. These are the highest nuchal line, the precondylar
tubercle, and the posterior ethmoid foramen. Seventy-eight skulls were examined for these conditions. Of the 14 revealing the highest nuchal line, 9
come from cluster C. Ten of the 15 crania with a precondylar tubercle and 11
of the 19 having a posterior ethmoid foramen are likewise from cluster C.
This encourages the idea that the traits are hereditary and that they were
transmitted through successive members of the same family line. It is also
noted that the posterior ethmoid foramen was present in three successive putative generations represented by female burials 109, 73, and 83, and again
with female burials 47 and 18. It is particularly interesting to find that the
male burials 90, 93, 72, and 67 also have this condition. Given its rarity in the
sample as a whole, it is suggested that its presence in males and females in
this group from burial 109 is more compatible with the males being siblings
rather than spouses of the females with whom they were interred. Again,
burials 79 and 77 are likely to contain sisters, or a mother and her daughter.

To a certain extent, the highest nuchal line presents a similar pattern, beginning with the male burial 131, and proceeding in at least one member of the succeeding four generations, including the male burials 72 and 67. The precondylar tubercle is present at the very beginning of the cluster with burial 140, and then occurs over five generations from burials 73 to 37. Two males, burials 72 and 67, reveal this condition. The presence of an open supra-orbital foramen or notch is found in members of nine succeeding generations from burial 109 down to one of the two females under the raised structure (B. 19). Burials 18 and 19 also have coronal wormian bones, which are present in the crania of burials 35, 45, 6, and 83. Only seven skeletons in the site have the astertonic bone, but two of these are burials 45 and 47, a finding that encourages their placement in Figure 3.6 as mother and daughter.

When we turn to the dentition, we encounter similar recurrences over several generations. The first five generations include individuals with a cingulum on the upper first incisor. Members of seven generations display a mesiolingual or "Carabelli's" cusp on the upper first molar. This feature also links burial 6 with the preceding burials 35 and 36.

We had also noticed that many of the adults and children had missing teeth. These conformed, in individuals, to a matching pattern, such as two incisors, or both upper and lower first molars. Rachanie considered the patterns of deliberate tooth removal in each cluster to see if each reveals a consistently different preference. Fourteen different categories based on the pattern of tooth evulsion were identified. In terms of different treatment applied to the males or females, it is clear that members of both sexes underwent tooth evulsion. The removal of both upper first incisors was the commonest pattern, with eight males and three females. The only apparently consistent sexually dimorphic pattern was the restriction of the removal of all the lower and the two upper first incisors to women. There appears to have been a development in terms of the preferred pattern of tooth evulsion with time. Groups 1–5 and 10–11 are found only during MP 2–4. If we exclude children, the absence of any evulsion is confined to MP 1–3. Thereafter, all adults had some of their teeth removed. Groups 7–9, all of which involved the removal of the upper or lower incisor row, tended to be later.

It is possible that the pattern of tooth evulsion varies between clusters. If clusters reflect social groupings, then tooth removal could be seen as an affiliative marker. There are hints that such differences occur. Group 2 concentrates in cluster F ($n = 4$), with one example respectively in clusters A and C. Group 4 was particularly favored with cluster C, with only one burial in cluster F revealing the extraction of the second upper incisors

It is interesting to note that, in terms of the pattern of tooth evulsion for cluster C, no teeth were removed from any of the first four generation members, male or female. Pattern 4, that involving the removal of both upper second incisors, was found in two males (Bs. 131 and 72) and two females (Bs. 64 and 77). Burial 45 revealed pattern 9 (involving all upper and lower incisors), while successively burials 35, 36, and 18 had pattern 8, in which all four lower incisors and the upper first incisors were removed. Given the

number of options open, it is held that the consistency of this pattern involving males and females is compatible with the notion of specified markers for successive members of the same family line.

Cluster F also reveals a continuity of burials during MP 2–4. In Figure 3.6,
a proposed genealogy is set out, including both burials 14–16 and the members of cluster H. There is less consistency in the pattern of tooth evulsion
than might be expected, and less than was observed for cluster C. Nevertheless, pattern 2 was present in burials 40, 39, 38, and 29, while for burials 15,
13, and 4, which reveal patterns 6, 9, and 7 respectively, there is in common
the complete extraction of either the lower or upper incisor row, or both.

Since it was evident that pottery-making was undertaken throughout the
occupation, we wondered if each group retained its own preferences for pottery styles and decoration. Dianne Hall took up this theme for her master's
research. Finally, Rachanie began to look very closely at the way in which
people were buried within each of the two durable clusters to try to identify
consistent differences between them. Dianne Hall could not identify any design motifs on the pottery that were particularly prevalent in or exclusive to
one of the clusters, but Rachanie was able to show that adults and infants interred in close proximity had some singular features of the mortuary ritual
in common (Fig. 3.7).

THE PEOPLE OF KHOK PHANOM DI

One of the most important potential sources of information about prehistoric communities is the remains of the people themselves. There are
many sites in Southeast Asia where soil conditions do not allow the preservation of bone, and this seriously reduces the degree to which the society itself can be assessed. At Khok Phanom Di, however, we had the good fortune
to encounter excellent conditions, not only for the survival of the bone itself,
but also the complete nature of most of the interments. Hardly any had been
disturbed by later activity. We were also very careful in the field to pack all
the material for shipping with care to minimize damage in transit. When the
human remains arrived in the laboratory of the Department of Anatomy in
Dunedin, many months were spent in cleaning and restoring the bones. This
sample is, therefore, one of the largest and certainly the best provenanced
from Southeast Asia.

Bone is a relatively plastic medium, in that it grows and responds to the
demands placed upon it. Muscle is attached to bone via tendons. The places
where the tendons are anchored into the bone may be placed under considerable stress, and ridges of bone form at insertion points to cope with such
demands. Nutrition also affects the robustness of bones, while traumas during growth may cause the formation of lines of arrested growth, known as
Harris lines. The teeth are also a most important source of information on
the prehistoric diet, and we have already seen how individuals are likely to
inherit specific skeletal features from their parents. One of the most common
questions asked of the skeletal remains is "what did this person die of." This

FIGURE 3.7   *Burial 99 in the center contains a woman aged in her mid-forties at death. It is suggested that the 7- to 8-month-old beside her is her child. Note that the pottery vessels are placed in a corresponding position over the knees. The burial to the right is a male who also died in his mid-forties and is interpreted as her son.*

is not easily answered, although the skeleton is affected by some diseases which would have caused chronic ill health, such as yaws and syphilis. If the bones are sufficiently well preserved, it is also possible to identify a person's sex, approximate age at death, stature, and body mass.

All these avenues of inquiry have been followed by Nancy Tayles, and it is due to her work that it is now possible to incorporate human health and demography into this consideration of what happened at Khok Phanom Di (Tayles 1992). She found that the earliest six people, two men, a woman and three infants, were relatively tall and had good, strong bone development. Despite this evidence of a more than adequate diet, one man died when about 20, the woman at about 25, and the second man survived until the late thirties. Why should people have died so young, and why did half the individuals in this earliest phase succumb at birth or soon thereafter? Nancy noted changes in the skull, involving a thickening of the bone of the vault, which was very probably the result of anemia. One infant and the two younger adults showed evidence of this condition, the most likely cause being thalassemia. This blood disorder, while associated with anemia, also provides partial resistance to the malarial mosquito. It is fatal to an infant if both parents are afflicted, but if only one parent suffers, the infant will normally survive. The earliest adults at this site also suffered from periodontal disease, and the diet was sufficiently abrasive to cause considerable tooth wear. This may well have been due to the number of shellfish consumed.

One of the most important aspects of the sample of burials is that infants were interred in a similar manner as adults. It seems likely, therefore, that we have a reasonable chance of actually ascertaining the level of infant mortality. During MP2, for example, 55 percent of all 56 individuals died before reaching one year of age. Only 19 of these people reached adulthood. Again, thalassemia was present but was mainly among the young. Nancy Tayles has identified much evidence for a disruption in normal growth patterns and relatively poor bone development among males. It is also most interesting to note that the males suffered from degeneration among the joints of the back, neck, shoulders, lower back, hands, and legs. Three of these men suffered such problems only on the right side. It seems that they had regular and vigorous use of their limbs, particularly concentrated in the upper body. Women, on the other hand, did not suffer in this respect. Remarkably, the women and men also showed different tooth wear and incidence of caries, suggesting that their diets were dissimilar.

The sex ratio in MP3 is almost equal, there being nine women and ten men. Again, a very high proportion (54.8%) of the 42 burials came from infants, 20 dying at or very soon after birth. The men were taller and more robust than at any other phase. Their bones were also well developed, although the same pattern of joint degeneration continued and thalassemia persisted. There were some intriguing changes during MP4. Infant mortality appears to have fallen considerably. There were, however, more graves containing children, four out of the five showing evidence for having suffered from anemia. The men suffered a decline in health. They were smaller, less robust, and died at a younger age than their predecessors. They also show a markedly reduced incidence of degeneration of the joints. The teeth were also more healthy: there was less evidence for caries and periodontal disease, due in all probability to dietary change.

The last three mortuary phases contain only a further 21 individuals. Again, the number of new-born infants represented is low, but the number of child burials remains quite high. Men continued to be relatively free of joint degeneration, and adult teeth show little wear or periodontal disease, although many suffered from caries. Men and women were shorter and less robust during this final period of the cemetery. Throughout the sequence, women seem to have pursued the same activity pattern that affected the joints of the knees and lower back, but from MP4, men were relatively inactive compared with their predecessors.

Nancy Tayles, in summarizing her findings, has stressed the clarity of the change in health, activity patterns, diet, and lowered infant mortality which occurred when comparing MP4 with the earlier remains.

ILLUMINATING SOCIAL ORGANIZATION

After two years of reconstructing the human remains, obtaining the life histories of 154 prehistoric people, counting beads, assessing tooth extraction patterns, and many other preliminaries, we began to approach the principal aim of our work, the way in which this society was ordered over a period of about twenty generations. We had at our disposal some basic information on each individual. For adults, we knew their sex and approximate age at death. The sex of children and infants cannot at present be ascertained. We knew their place in a chronological sequence, broadly defined in seven mortuary phases. We could catalogue the pattern of tooth extraction and whether or not they were interred with red ochre. Then there were the grave goods. Shell jewelry was the most common, particularly beads of several varieties: the disc, barrel, I, cylinder, and H-shaped. Next came pottery vessels. Then there were clay anvils and burnishing stones, implements which could have been used for shaping and decorating pots and buried with their owner at death. Some anvils bear incised designs which might have been ownership marks. Carved turtle carapace ornaments were found in later graves, and some artifacts were rare. Few people had stone adzeheads, fishhooks, or pierced animal teeth. Other items were unique, such as the Nautilus shell or the shark spine. Sifting through these variables with a pencil and paper produced some possible leads. H-shaped beads were late; barrel beads were early. The quantity of shell disc beads varied sharply with time. The analysis, however, required the application of multivariate statistics, for there were too many graves and variables for the human brain to evaluate properly.

Bryan Manly, Professor of Mathematics at the University of Otago, had helped in previous studies, and it was to him that we turned for further advice. We asked him to consider several issues. First, was any cluster consistently richer, in terms of grave goods, than any other? The reason for this question reflects a considerable number of cases where, at least in recent mortuary behavior, it has been found that the treatment of a dead person is a reflection of that person's social position when alive. Funerary rites and practices are conducted by the living, and they often are designed to project their perceived place in society. An individual who had wide influence and range of contacts might also attract people from other communities to the funeral, and the provision of feasts in honor of the dead are a further means of obtaining prestige, for the magnificence and duration of the proceedings sends out signals on the status of the hosts. There are numerous instances where this relationship does not work. Very wealthy people might, for religious reasons, be interred in simple graves. But it is necessary for the prehistorian to consider his material in as much detail as possible in order to weigh alternative interpretations. We therefore wished to find out if the community at Khok Phanom Di ever comprised two groups of unequal wealth. If it did, it would suggest a situation of social inequality.

We then turned to the treatment accorded males and females. Were members of either sex consistently differentiated in some way? Could we identify a changing relationship in which men or women came to dominate the social life of the community? Where anthropologists can study modern communities, they are invariably drawn to the kinship system and the social roles played by its members. Geoffrey Benjamin has spent much time considering kinship among the peoples of Malaysia, and has stressed the contrast between a patri- and a matri-pole. In the former, males tend to dominate and determine decision making, but in the latter, it is the women who rise in prominence. In a patrilineal community that is exogamous, women will leave on marriage, and women from another place will be introduced as brides. A matrifocal group, however, would tend to retain young women in their community of birth. In some groups, men can strive through personal prowess or success in accumulating prestige and followers, to become big men, leaders. Yet their sons may not inherit such status. Less common, but not unknown, are systems in which individual women can obtain personal prestige, wealth, and status through their own endeavors. On the other hand, some groups do ascribe status to the children of leaders, heralding inbuilt inequality within the system.

A possible way of identifying such inequality is to find infants or children who were given opulent burials, on the premise that they could not have achieved the social prestige consistent with such treatment during their brief lives. This might be true in some cases, but it is equally possible that parents might wish to further their own social aspirations by according their offspring an impressive funeral. We therefore asked Brian Manly to look at the way in which the young were treated in death. This approach, for example, would aim to identify whether young people were unusually richly endowed only when interred with rich adults.

There are many dimensions to social behavior, and we wished to follow as many leads as possible. We therefore turned to the question of age. If individuals sought status and social prominence, could a longer lifespan have increased their opportunity of doing so? Were older people normally richer, in terms of grave goods, than younger adults?

THE STATISTICAL ANALYSIS OF THE BURIALS

There are several statistical analyses which could be applied to our data, and with Bryan Manly's advice and help, we employed those which we thought would best resolve the social issues that interested us. First, we subdivided the artifacts found in the graves into three groups: ornaments, utilitarian, and symbolic items. Naturally, some ornaments might also have been symbolic and vice versa. Ornaments included necklaces, belts, bracelets, bangles, anklets, and pendants. The most common raw material was shell; the most abundant artifact, the bead. Disc beads were found throughout. Other forms came and went with time. Other jewelry types, such as pendants, were usually made from mammalian canines. We noted that these were normally associated with rather rich graves, for example burials 132, 43, 33, and 15. Utilitarian items are those which had clear technological uses, such as clay anvils, burnishing stones, bone fishhooks, polished stone adze-heads, clay anvils, and clay net sinkers. Many of these items had clearly been used before interment. The symbolic items include the pottery vessels and ornamented turtle carapaces. Many of the pottery vessels were of a form rarely encountered in non-mortuary context, and they were more often decorated. Both the pots and carapaces were often found smashed or "killed" as part of the mortuary rites.

The first series of tests involved multiple regression analysis. Because of the great range of items found in graves, from nothing to over 100,000, the base was not the raw number of artifacts, but the logarithm of the number of each type plus 1. It was found that there was considerable variation in the presence or absence of some types with time. In terms of overall wealth, there was an early peak in MP2, then a decline in MP 3–4 followed by a sharp rise in MP5 and then another decline in MP 6–7. In this test, there does not seem to have been a significant difference in overall wealth between males and females, nor between either sex and children. Infants, however, were in general poorer in terms of grave goods than females.

In order to examine trends and specific comparisons between groups of graves, we then ran an average-link hierarchic cluster analysis using Jaccard's coefficient of similarity. This fearsome-sounding procedure expresses the distance between individual interments, and is appropriate where, as at Khok Phanom Di, there are many missing values. Some graves, for example, have no associated artifacts at all. We ran this statistic using not only artifacts, but the type of tooth evulsion pattern identified, the presence or absence of red ochre, and of a shroud. The result of this analysis is a dendrogram in which graves are located close to each other if they are similar, and increasingly remotely as difference increases. That in figure 3.8, for example, shows the results for an analysis of males and females in MP2. The question is, were males and females treated differently in death? The answer is apparently not, for the two broad groupings identified comprise males and females in the ratios of 4:4 and 4:6. One of the groups had few grave goods at all, the other had shell beads and pots.

Similar tests run on other sets of burials showed that males and females continued to be buried in a similar fashion during MP3, but during MP4, a group was identified comprising only males, all being found with turtle carapace ornaments. We then turned our attention to infants, which in this case included all individuals dying before they attained about 3 years of age. There was considerable variation in the way they were treated. Twenty-two infants were left out because they had no grave goods of any sort. The first group of twenty analysed burials was found only with a dusting of red ochre and fragments of a shroud. Other groups were distinguished on the basis of possessing fish vertebrae bangles, those with a small number of shell beads, two graves (16 and 33) with many shell beads, then a group of four early infant graves with moderate wealth. All belong to MP2; three are from cluster F, and the other from cluster B. They have in common shell beads and pottery vessels. The next group of ten infants had one or two pots and, in some cases, a few disc beads.

We thus can suggest four major groups of infant burials. The first had only its grave and its link with a given cluster. The second includes red ochre and a shroud. Next, we have those with a set of grave goods, which

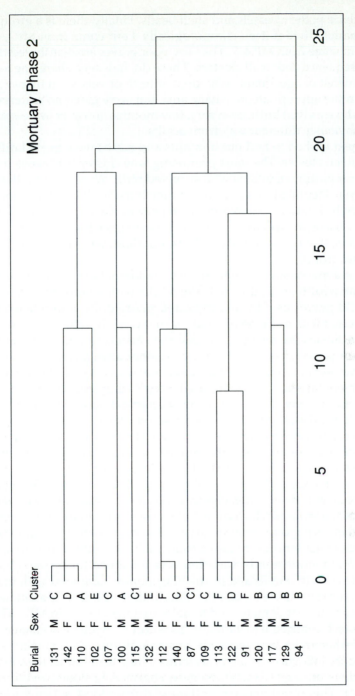

FIGURE 3.8 *The result of a cluster analysis applied to the males and females from mortuary phase 2 reveals no evidence for different treatment between the sexes.*

may include pottery vessels and shell beads. Finally, there is a group of rich graves which divides itself chronologically. Four come from MP2, and another four come from MP 4–7. The very poor graves are distributed throughout the sequence and in all clusters. These do, however, share one feature in common: that of age. Infants who died at birth or very soon thereafter were placed in the appropriate mortuary area, but were given no material items. Those who survived birth, even for a few months, however, were not treated in any obviously different way from adults.

We next wished to find out if infants and adults were treated differently in any given cluster. The most promising was cluster F, because it has the highest proportion of infants who survived birth. We found that the statistical analysis identified first a group of nine burials, all but one belonging to MP2, in which adults and infants were present. Each was buried with pots and shell beads irrespective of age. In cluster C, we found that infants who survived birth were linked with adults, but those who died at birth formed a separate group.

Few graves contained the remains of children. We found a clear link between the wealth of children and the adults with whom they were buried. Poor child graves usually accompanied poor adults, and where children were interred with a rich set of goods, so too were the adults alongside them.

It has already been suggested that the clusters might represent distinct social groups. We decided to inquire whether any cluster is distinguished from any other in terms of the mortuary rite, with particular reference to the inclusion of grave goods. For this analysis, all adults were included. The test failed to isolate any particular cluster as being differentially rich up to the end of MP4, although thereafter the situation changed dramatically.

It would be unwise to rely on the results of one type of statistical analysis. The clustering provided us with some intriguing results, but further testing was necessary. For this, Bryan Manly produced another fearsome-sounding statistic, a principal component analysis with varimax rotation being applied to the five components with eigenvalues in excess of 1.0. Essentially, this highlights the artifacts which contribute most to variability and therefore differences between groups or individuals. However, we had to remove rare objects from consideration because their inclusion might lead to spurious results. We found that most variation was accounted for by the contrast between graves with anvils and burnishing stones, compared with those that included turtle carapace ornaments. This finding also reflects a difference between the treatment of males and females first manifested in MP3. The other factors which contribute to variation all reflect chronological change in bead types. We therefore ran further tests, this time on successive mortuary phases to reduce the influence of temporal change. They highlighted the contrast between graves during MP3 with anvils and burnishing stones, and those without either. This result was strengthened during MP4, when graves with anvils stood in sharp contrast to those with turtle carapace ornaments.

A third and final statistic was then applied to the data. It is known as multidimensional scaling. In effect, this technique produces a "map" in two or three dimensions, which reflects the "distance" between two graves. Close proximity on the map equates with similar grave goods. Distance reflects dissimilarity. Viewed in two dimensions (Fig. 3.9), there is a large concentration of graves which have no grave goods. Graves become richer as they proceed towards a maximum value of −6.44 for dimension 1 (burial 15). There is also a temporal change, for graves with high positive values for dimension 2 contain the early shell barrel beads. Again, we ran the test on graves from MP2, and then on those from MP3–4, the latter combined due to insufficient numbers when taken singly.

The results for MP2 suggest three configurations. The first, where values for dimension 2 are all negative, reveals burials rising in terms of mortuary wealth as dimension 1 increases in value. The second has positive scores for dimension 2 and negative ones for dimension 1. This group contains five burials, three from cluster B and two from cluster D. Two are males and three, children. They all have barrel beads. Of these, burials 121, 129, and 130 lay beside each other. Burials 117 and 133 also lay beside each other in the square and on the multidimensional scaling map. The third grouping includes five burials, all belonging to cluster F; these are richer than the cluster B and D graves in that they include disc and barrel beads as well as pottery vessels. Once again, the graves in question are virtually contemporaneous and buried beside each other. There are three infants, a man, and a woman.

For MP3–4, there is a large concentration of burials with only one or two pottery vessels. But it sets apart burials 73, 90, and 93, which have barrel beads. These three were contemporary and lay adjacent to each other. Thus, when the chronological factor is eliminated, this sensitive technique tends to group together people buried contemporaneously in the same cluster. This is a most significant finding, for it tends to support our hypothesis that the clusters are made up of people who were related and shared similar preferences. It encouraged us to look at the way people were interred in even more detail.

Our first objective was to try to identify whether pottery vessels were placed in different ways with the dead of each cluster. We tabulated where each pot had been placed, whether it was on its base, upside down, or on its side, whether pots were complete or broken, and if the latter, whether the pieces formed a tight group or had been scattered deliberately over the body. We concluded that there was no consistent difference between any two clusters on the basis of the placement and treatment of pottery vessels as part of the mortuary ritual during MP2–4. On the other hand, there was a clear, overall pattern of change with time. During MP2, it was customary to place complete pots in the leg region. With MP3, there was a change in favor of broken vessels being placed in the region of the legs. A further change took place with MP4, when burials displayed greater variation in vessel placement than did those in any other cluster. The only hint of specific treatment within a given cluster has been detected for cluster F during MP4, when burials displayed greater variation in vessel placement than did contemporary burials in any other cluster. This might be the result of small sample size, but it is also possible that the cluster F people had their own preferences.

In terms of the placement of shell jewelry during MP2–4, we noted that only some members of cluster C were interred wearing clothing embroidered with shell disc beads. These individuals were buried near each other over a short timespan, and were also, with the exception of burial 109, buried with a

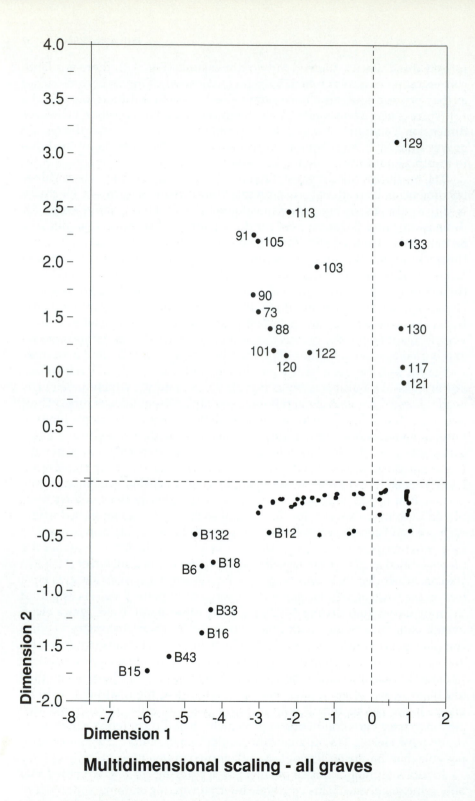

Multidimensional scaling - all graves

FIGURE 3.9 *The result of a multidimensional scaling, on this occasion using only two dimensions, for the Khok Phanom Di burials.*

relatively rich assemblage of well-decorated pottery vessels. Apart from this group of rich graves, there is no other clear evidence of a distinction between clusters on the basis of jewelry. Rather, there is a clear time trend. We find that MP2 graves were often well endowed with shell jewelry, but that the amount fell sharply over all clusters during MP3–4. Only one adult, a male (burial 132) in cluster E, stands out for its extreme wealth.

All clusters include burials associated with burnishing stones, but there is no distinction between them in terms of where they were placed. The only difference noted is that in the case of cluster F, they were found only with males, but in cluster C, all but one were found with females. Anvils were only found with women, children, and infants, the earliest being from an MP3 context. None was found in any cluster A, B, D, or E graves.

It has already been argued that the Jaccard analyses undertaken have failed clearly to identify any cluster during MP 2–4 which stood out as being unusually rich. When all the graves in each cluster are grouped for the purpose of the analyses, individuals and their associations with others tend to lose focus within the group. Yet it is argued that one of the more unusual features of the Khok Phanom Di cemetery is the fact that stages in the addition of bodies to collective burial areas are recognizable. This situation makes possible an examination of changes in mortuary practice in an unusually detailed manner.

In order to express the successive changes in the composition of sets of grave goods for each stage in a cluster, we decided to assign a given number of points to each type of grave offering. In doing so, we appreciated that this procedure is arbitrary and the figures might be expected to provide only a rough approximation at best to the relative wealth of graves. Emphasis has been given to whether the raw material used was exotic to the site, whether the artifact shows high skill in manufacture, and whether it was rare. While this procedure is arbitrary, our purpose is to show how the grave goods varied with the age at death of an individual, through time and between members of different clusters.

The number of grave goods per burial has been computed and average point scores for the burials comprising each cluster and stage have then been calculated beginning with MP2, clusters A, D, B, and C were much on a par, with point scores of between 0 and 172. Cluster E, which began slightly later than the other four, is very rich indeed (average 2089), but it is difficult to evaluate further because it is on the edge of the excavated area, and no subsequent stages have been identified. The second and third stages of cluster C remain within the range of 0–172 points, but in Stage 4, there was an increase to 436 points. The point score then fell over the next three stages down to 158, 147, and 67 and rose again significantly with the final stage in MP4 with a score of 251.

Cluster F presents a rather different sequence. Having begun with two quite wealthy stages, with scores of nearly 248 and 261, scores then became poorer, with all stages save the last having figures of under 200. During these last stages, the figure rose, along with that of the contemporary burials in cluster C, to 214 and 320, while the only burial comprising the final stage had no grave goods. Thus, as cluster C in Stage 4 became very rich, the contemporary interments in cluster F became poor. Cluster A, on the other hand, never rose above 185 points. It was always relatively poor. Cluster D presents a further pattern. It began by being very poor (no points), then rose to fair wealth, with scores of 326, 189, and 284, at the same time that cluster C during Stages 5–6 shows a declining trend. Either due to the sampling difficulties encountered at the edge of the square, or to cultural reasons we can only speculate about at present, cluster D then ceased, although the single burial ascribed to Stage 5, which was found 2 meters higher, might be linked with this cluster.

There are several possible interpretations of oscillating wealth through the putative generations. They will be considered below.

INDIVIDUAL WEALTH

In order to assess differences in wealth between individuals, we gave each grave an individual point score using our formula. In the main, each phase provides a similar pattern. The majority of graves have fewer than 300 points. There is also a much smaller group of wealthier graves, with scores of over 500 points. For MP2, this includes a very rich adult male, with a score of 7956, three infants, and another male. Three of these rich burials come from cluster F, one from D, and the last from cluster E. For MP3, there are two males and a female, all from cluster C, Stages 4 and 5. Only one grave exceeds a score of 500 during MP4, that of an infant with a score of 2309. It does not belong to any cluster. With MP5, the graves became very much richer, B15 having a score of 26,968. Burial 43, a male, scored 12,265, while the infant burials 14 and 16 scored 454 and 3190 respectively. During MP6, the graves under the structure had scores of 861, 2714, and 4336 respectively, even though two were found in a disturbed condition. Those belonging to cluster H in front of the structure scored 461, 502, 300, 501, 100, and 60, with two infants scoring 0. Perhaps significantly, the cluster H burials could only muster 13 disc beads between them against almost 30,000 for the three graves under the structure. The three MP7 graves had scores of 576, 540, and 633.

WERE OLDER PEOPLE MORE WEALTHY?

We then considered the possibility that mortuary wealth was structured, at least in part, according to the age of the deceased. The figures produced from this exercise suggest that a person's age was not a determining factor in the provision of grave goods. In Figure 3.10, the relationship between wealth, age, and sex is shown. While it is evident that women tended to outlive men, there is no clear signal that either age or sex were associated with more wealth in terms of grave goods.

CRAFT SPECIALIZATION

Khok Phanom Di was a pottery-making center throughout its prehistoric occupation. This is indicated not only by evidence for clay preparation, the

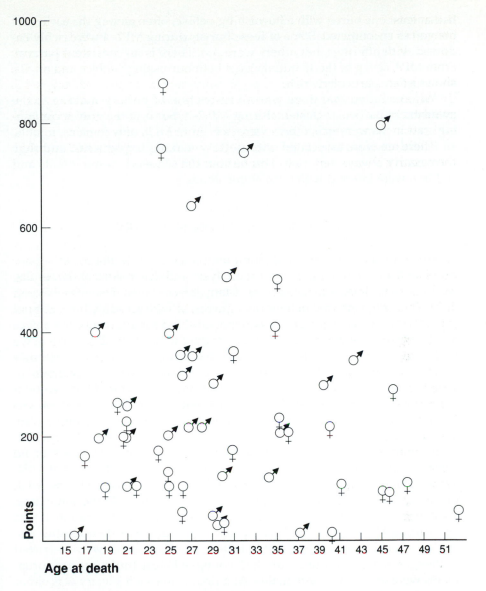

FIGURE 3.10   *The relationship between age, sex, and mortuary wealth among the adults from Khok Phanom Di.*

shaping and decorating of pots, and probably their firing, but also by the presence of both clay anvils and burnishing pebbles in some of the graves. We therefore inquired whether special treatment was accorded craft specialists, if that was the status of those buried with the implements used to fashion and decorate pots. Anvils, clay cylinders, and burnishing pebbles only appeared in mortuary contexts from MP4 (with the exception of the doubtful association of B82). They were restricted to the burials of females, infants, and children, and the few graves in question were, with one exception, very rich. Burnishing pebbles were found in association with the graves of eleven females, six males, three infants, and four children. It is notable that all clusters had at least one burial with a burnishing pebble, often among the earliest of the graves encountered. Some of these burials during MP2–4 were richly endowed with offerings, but others were not. There is no consistent pattern. From MP4, seven of the 15 burials have both burnishing pebbles and anvils, and most are particularly rich.

We concluded that there was no restriction of pottery-making to the members of particular clusters during MP 2–4. Some of the graves containing craft items were rich, others were not. From MP5, only females, infants, and children were associated with pottery-making implements, and they were nearly always very rich. Throughout the sequence, some infants and children were interred with burnishing stones.

SOCIAL ORGANIZATION: SUMMARY

We approached Bryan Manly with only hazy ideas on the social organization at Khok Phanom Di. After his analyses and discussions of the results, we felt able to draw some inferences. Many infants failed to survive beyond birth. They were interred in their own graves, or with an adult, but were not provided with grave goods. Those who survived for a few months before dying, however, were given the same treatment as adults. For MP2–4, we failed to find any consistent evidence that any cluster was consistently richer than any other. However, there were instances where individuals interred at the same stage in one cluster stood out on account of the wealth of their grave goods. This is seen in cluster C with burials 73, 90, and 93. The first stage of cluster E saw a man and woman of unusual wealth interred together. The early cluster F burials (101, 105, 112, and 113) were all provided with copious shell beads and some pottery vessels. There was, however, no consistent association of wealth with a given cluster up to the end of MP4. Yet we did encounter two intriguing trends during this span. During MP4, the amount of shell jewelry dwindled to almost nothing. At the same time, the pottery vessels were less varied in form and plainer in decoration. It was also during MP4 that the multivariate statistical analyses detected the first evidence for differential treatment of the sexes. Clay anvils were restricted to the graves of some women and the young, whereas turtle carapace ornaments were only found with males. At a time when shell jewelry was either in short supply or no longer sought after in mortuary ritual, women were interred with the implements for making pottery vessels.

Mortuary phase 5 represents a sharp dislocation, yet there remained elements of continuity. The orientation, the use of red ochre, the continued interment of anvils with a woman and the young were maintained. But we also encounter a whole new range of artifacts and a quantity of grave goods that almost stretches credibility. Shell was now converted into large discs, bracelets, ear ornaments, and a new variety of bead fashioned in the shape of an I. Clay cylinders were heaped on two bodies, much more red ochre was used, and new forms of richly ornamented pottery vessels appeared alongside the established varieties. Yet this wealth was a brief episode for cluster F, for the following generations had few grave goods. In clusters C and F, we also find that from MP4, women predominated. Two women were interred in association with the raised structure, both with clay anvils. In the former, we encountered only women in the last seven suggested generations. We cannot explain this absence of males. Yet the predominance of women may well reflect an increasing matrilocal aspect to the later people at Khok Phanom Di. Some of them were interred with considerable opulence.

In 1988, we offered a preliminary interpretation. We suggested that the association of clay anvils with women, and with some infants or children, was highly significant. If Khok Phanom Di was a trading community, then women could aspire to high status by fashioning quality pots and exchanging them for exotic, prestige goods. In a book on Melanesian exchange, we found references to just such a system operating in living memory on the Louisade Archipelago (Lepowsky 1983). If potting skills were passed from one generation of women to the next, then it would have been increasingly necessary to keep the rising generation of potters in the community. This would in turn stress the matri-pole. If no girls survived to the next generation, then a family itself would come to an end. Our minds went back to the remains of a 15-month-old interred with such riches next to the Princess, and in particular to the tiny anvil placed beside the right ankle.

This interpretation seemed plausible at the time. But the results of other analyses were becoming available, and these expanded our knowledge of the people of Khok Phanom Di and enabled us to obtain deeper insight into their ritual of death.

4

The Biological Remains

In regions with a longer history of archaeological inquiry, the analysis of fossil pollen has been a standard way of reconstructing prehistoric environments and for assessing the human impact on the vegetation. The application of this technique in conjunction with prehistoric sites in mainland Southeast Asia has seldom been undertaken, and we were, therefore, delighted and intrigued when Bernard Maloney arrived in Bangkok, armed with a core borer, to join us. He began to assemble a collection of all the plant species that grew in the vicinity of the site, and at the same time, sought likely swampy places where he could sink his borer and remove cores of sediment for analysis. This project required the assistance of two strong men, who forced the implement into the ground at half meter increments. After removing the collecting head, a sample of the sediment was extracted, placed into polythene, and the procedure was repeated. Some of his cores reached a depth of 7 meters before they encountered a white, hard clay that proved to be impenetrable.

Cores were taken from all round the site, and they ended up in Maloney's laboratory in Belfast. Then began the painstaking task of describing the sediments in terms of how they accumulated. Most of the material was a green clay, which was probably laid down under a shallow sea, confirming many findings that the sea level was higher than at present, and it was during this phase that many meters of such clay accumulated. In KL2, the name given to a core taken north of the site, the marine clay was overlain by a gray clay, which represents a phase of dry land and soil formation. This in turn was followed by the accumulation of brown and green clays, the latter appearing as a very narrow band, possibly representing a brief marine transgression. A lens of black clay at a depth of only 0.82 meters below the ground surface also represents a marine transgression.

How does this sequence of deposits relate to the nearby site? This question has been answered by extracting samples of charcoal from two of the cores and dating them at Oxford University, where accelerator mass spectroscopy makes possible the dating of extremely small samples. The point in the sequence at the top of the green marine clay was dated to between 5800–4755 B.C., thus confirming that the early marine transgression took place in this area well before 4500 B.C. This deposit took place at a depth of 5 meters. A date of 4710–3960 B.C. was obtained at a depth of 2.25 meters, again much earlier than the adjacent site. At a depth of just under 0.91 meters, however, the date obtained, 1910–1435 B.C., matches that for the prehistoric settlement, although it should be mentioned that there is a second date from half a meter lower that dates to only about 550 years ago, and might have been contaminated in some way. The date obtained from another core, at a depth of just under a meter, is 2855–2185 B.C.

Maloney recovered pollen grains, fern spores, microscopic fragments of charcoal, and leaf fragments from successive sections of each core, and these have allowed him to reconstruct the vegetational history of the area before the site was occupied (Maloney 1991). The pollen from the green clay is dominated by mangrove species, indicating that, until about 4300 B.C., the coring location was under the sea, or at the very least in the intertidal zone. Maloney also detected a number of instances where there was a rise in grass pollen, charcoal concentrations, and the pollen from plants which are known, today, to flourish in rice fields. Unfortunately, it is not possible to ascribe grass pollen with certainty to rice, but the size and surface patterning of the pollen associated with the high charcoal readings is at least consistent with the presence of rice. These episodes date to about 5300, 5000, and 4300 B.C. They could reflect fortuitous conflagrations in the vicinity of the coring area, or perhaps deliberate firing by groups of hunter–gatherers in order to encourage grass growth and attract game animals. A third alternative is that one or more such episodes might be the result of deliberate clearance of the natural vegetation by fire in order to create conditions suited to rice cultivation. We are not able to resolve this issue, nor will it be possible until prehistoric sites dated to the same timespans are identified and examined. In the case of Khok Phanom Di itself, there are high readings of grass pollen and charcoal thought to equate with its occupation. Maloney has suggested that the site was located in the intertidal zone, and that rice may have been cultivated on its landward side.

OSTRACODES AND FORAMS

The last two weeks of the excavation involved drawing and sampling all the sections, undertaken by Charles Higham and Glen Standring (Fig. 4.1). We had decided to take a sample of every single context, which ran to hundreds for each of the four sides of the square. Bernard Maloney had been in correspondence with an Australian expert on ostracodes and forams, tiny aquatic species many of which have a restricted habitat. It seemed to us that such creatures might have been present at Khok Phanom Di, so we wrote to Ken McKenzie, asking him to look at some of the samples we had taken. At the same time, Bernard sent some samples taken from his pollen cores. His initial impression, on treating and examining our samples, was pessimistic. But once he looked at the material at 60 times magnification, he began to recognize both forams and ostracodes. Since these are so small, and could only have reached the site naturally or fortuitously, they are potentially a rich source of environmental information. Their comparative rarity, however, suggested that the site was never actually inundated by the sea, rather the specimens blew in on the wind, or were brought in attached to something larger, such as plants or shells. The actual species identified show that the site was located on or near an estuary, backed by freshwater marshes. In time, however, more brackish water conditions prevailed as the sea retreated from the site. An important sample from Layer 8 also contained ostracodes that cannot tolerate brackish water, indicating freshwater ponds were within reach of the site. McKenzie has suggested that the environment for these species could well have been rice fields.

ANIMAL BONES

Thousands of fragments of bone were found, as well as the remains of crustacea. These had to be sorted into major groups in the laboratory: fish, mammal, bird, crab, and turtle. This task was not difficult, but rather time-consuming. We then had to find specialists prepared to analyze them. Fortunately, Amphan Kijngam was able to come to Dunedin to work on the fish, crabs, and turtles. Alan Grant, then a final year honors student, was looking for a topic for his honors dissertation, and agreed to take on the analysis of the larger mammalian bones under the supervision of Charles Higham. This

FIGURE 4.1   *One of the final tasks was to draw and sample the sections. This was undertaken by Charles Higham and Glen Standring.*

left the really difficult bird bone. Fortunately, I (CH) had given a lecture in London on Khok Phanom Di in 1985, and was approached afterwards by Barbara West, a specialist on bird bones from the Museum of London, to offer help with identifying the avifauna. I got in touch, and she kindly agreed to help, not only with the bird bone, but also with the many bones of species from rats to rhinoceros for which we had no comparative data.

She wrote regularly informing us of her progress on the other side of the world in the British Museum. She found that some species were restricted to the later layers while others were only found in those which built up during the life of the cemetery. The remains of crocodile, never common, were found in early contexts, as were the bones of the crane, ibis, or spoonbill, Oriental darter, and cormorant. The later part of the burial sequence saw the bones of the pelican and heron. These birds are adapted to marshland and mangrove conditions. The stork and Sarus crane are attracted to swamps and marshes, while the cormorant is only found in the earliest layers and prefers life on the open coast, in contrast to the Oriental darter, which likes to perch in trees and fish in calm rivers. These marine and riverine species were replaced in the post-mortuary layers by the crow and dusky broadbill, birds of woodland and forest. The porcupine and bandicoot also appeared in this late context, both preferring dry conditions.

Amphan Kijngam was able to identify a wide variety of fish, some from the estuary and others from freshwater habitats. One of the most common in the earlier layers is known as *Lates calcarifer*, a species that enters estuaries to spawn in May, before the monsoon breaks. They are usually caught on hooks or in traps, because they have sharp fin spines which sever or damage nets. Larger fish may attain a weight of 30 kilograms. The numbers of bones from these fish fell quite markedly from Layers 7 and 8. Tachysurid catfish also occupy river estuaries. Again, numbers fell sharply in Layers 5–7, and rose again in the uppermost cultural contexts. Rays were found in some abundance during Layers 10–11, fell in Layers 5–8, and rose again at the end of the sequence. By contrast the freshwater catfish of the genus *Clarias* was rarely seen in Layers 10–11, but rose in frequency in Layers 6 and 8. These fish are particularly well adapted to living in freshwater swamps, conditions matched in rice fields. Many thousands of fragments of the mangrove crab *Scylla serrata* were identified, the numbers declining progressively from Layer 9 onwards. A second coastal crab, *Portunus pelagicus*, was abundant in Layer 10 with 1233 claw fragments, but by Layer 7 was no longer found. This change follows a pattern, in which estuarine species predominated in the earlier part of the sequence, but then fell away in favor of freshwater fish.

The analysis of larger mammal bones showed that the inhabitants, able as they were to exploit the naturally abundant fish and other marine resources, were not concerned with raising domestic stock. Two species are relatively more abundant than any other, the macaque and the pig. There are insufficient bones from the latter to make it possible to determine whether they came from domestic or wild animals, but in either case, the few large animals represented show that they had little importance as a source of food. During the mortuary phases, the only other large mammals found are cattle, water buffalo, various types of deer, the langur, and the dog. The dog is the only definitely domestic animal. Prehistoric Thai domestic dogs are descended from the wolf, which is not native to tropical Southeast Asia. The closest possible source is the Chinese wolf. The presence of these dog bones, therefore, demonstrates some form of contact with China. Taken as a group, the other large mammals are interesting because they are all species which are known to raid rice fields in Southeast Asia today, and are therefore commonly trapped. The crab-eating macaque is also a native of mangrove forests, and the pig is known to enter mangroves. All the mammals became more common after the last mortuary phase.

THE SHELLFISH

Khok Phanom Di yielded the remains of over a million shellfish. It was quite impossible to transport them all to the laboratory for analysis, so we arranged to count the number of specimens from the most common species, the cockle *Anadara granosa,* in the field and retain 10 percent of them. All others were shipped to Dunedin. Even with a small proportion of the entire assemblage, housing them was difficult and arranging for their analysis was more so. Initially, Emily Glover in London kindly agreed to help, but the logistics and expense of shipping the specimens, together with the fact that a graduate student in New Zealand asked if she could begin the analysis, meant that she graciously appreciated my dilemma. The student then found another topic, leaving us with our original problem. Graeme Mason, a colleague who had spent many years building up our comparative faunal collections, and who had previously collected some shell material in Thailand, then offered to help. There followed four years of full-time research on the collection, leading to a report on all the 119 larger species identified.

Mason's first task was to ascribe each specimen to a species. Fortunately, we had already attempted a preliminary sort in the field, and one after another, the bags were opened and the contents laid out for more detailed scrutiny. On many occasions, a set would be put aside until literature on the family could be obtained from overseas. By the end of 1990, only a few difficult specimens were left, and Mason began to piece together the habitat preferences of the species represented, obtain an impression of the sort of environment which existed near Khok Phanom Di, and assess how it changed with time.

Anadara granosa was easily the most common species found. It is adapted to mudflats, and is found densely distributed in estuarine locations. The next most abundant is another bivalve, *Meretrix lusoria,* which prefers a sheltered, sandy habitat. The dominance of food as the reason for collecting shellfish is also revealed by the fact that only eight of the species identified, all known as sources of food, comprise 99.4 percent of the sample. Some of the other species probably colonized and lived on the site, while one of the freshwater bivalves, *Pseudodon,* was nearly always modified into an artifact. Still other species were preferred as raw materials for jewelry or as ornaments. Cowrie shells, for example, were usually found as grave goods. It is also likely that some shells entered the site as passengers on other goods, such as gathered plants. Mason noted, for example, that such plants as lotus and watercress are consumed today, and freshwater snails clinging to their stalks could have been introduced into the site accidentally.

Having identified as many of the specimens to their species as possible, Graeme Mason then sought information on their habitats. Some useful points were obtained from the literature, but the best source of information came from his own fieldwork, tracking down shellfish living today in a range of habitats in central Thailand. This took him to modern mangrove forests, freshwater ponds, dry rocky habitats, and to the island of Kho Si Chang in the Gulf of Siam. Eventually, he was able to reconstruct a number of distinct habitats from which the shells at Khok Phanom Di would have been obtained. We have already seen that the most common food species live in mudflats affected by tidal flows. Sixteen genera came from this rich habitat of estuarine muds. There would also have been clean, sheltered sandflats within reach of the site. Seven bivalves came from such an area, as well as the gastropods which prey upon them. Some of the species found come from a coral habitat. They require water with very low amounts of sediment, to allow the coral to establish itself, and Mason has suggested that such a habitat could have been present offshore. A few pieces of coral were found at the site itself. The seaward-facing mangrove forest has a series of distinct environmental niches, such as the mud at the base, the trunks of the trees, and their leafy canopy. Shell species from all these are found at the site. As tidal influence reduces further from the shore, mangrove species themselves change. The new range of shell adapted to drier middle or landward mangrove are also represented in the sample. Then there were also some species which are to be found in the estuary proper. One, *Coecella horsfieldi*, prefers estuarine sandbars. Not all the shells found, however, were marine or coastal. An important group comes from freshwater habitats, including running streams and still lakes. Finally, there was a group of snails that live on dry land. Yet Graeme Mason's study is confined to the larger species. More detailed information will be available only when he has completed his analysis of the very small shells which were obtained through our flotation machine.

By the middle of 1991, we had 119 shell species identified from about 750,000 specimens from 64 successive contexts at the site. Some were present in the thousands and others were represented by only one or two shells. Mason and I (CH) met often to discuss the next step, which was highly influenced by a very tight schedule for the completion of the next volume of our report. It seemed essential to seek the advice once again of Bryan Manly at the Mathematics Department. It was a very busy teaching term for him, and we had only a few weeks in which to finalize the report. He seemed intrigued by the statistical problems involved, and Mason and I soon found ourselves in his office, explaining what we sought of the raw data. We asked him if he could identify statistically significant time trends in the total number of species at the site. Then, are there time trends in the appearance of each species? We wanted to know if there were changes with time in the representation of each of the different habitats and finally, are there distinct groups of shellfish that reveal a similar habitat preference which also co-vary with time? One of the first problems he pointed out was that the sample was heavily weighted in terms of one species, *Anadara granosa*. Consequently, we concentrated on whether a species was simply present or absent from a given layer.

Having posed the questions, we settled down to an anxious wait. But Bryan was soon on the phone with the first results. There was a significant rise in the number of species represented, starting with relatively few, then increasing during the earlier parts of the mortuary sequence before falling again during MP4. There was then a sharp rise during MP6 before the numbers fell to only one or two species in Layer 3. He also found that the successive chronological contexts tend to have similar assemblages of species. Now came the really significant issue. Assuming that changing habitats in the vicinity of the site are reflected in the presence or absence of species from those habitats in the collection, to what extent can we track environmental changes with time?

This study proved more difficult than would seem from a superficial consideration, for some species can live in more than one habitat. Bryan Manly applied an ingenious scheme for coping with this problem, involving the partial allocation of a species to the range of habitats to which it is known to be adaptive. This procedure resulted in a set of graphs portraying the distribution of species assigned to given habitats through time. Trends were made clearer by presenting the running mean for four successive contexts. Graeme Mason was now close to identifying an environmental change which was to transform our understanding of the social changes represented by the mortuary sequence.

ENVIRONMENTAL CHANGE

The number of species associated with marine intertidal mud reached a peak during MP2, fell steadily during MP3 to a lower level, and then remained constant until the end of the life of the cemetery. Clean intertidal sand was not strongly represented in the lowest deposits, but species became very common during MP2–3, fell dramatically between MP3–4, and then rose slightly in numbers during the later part of the burial sequence. Shells from the clean coral habitat show a similar trend. The species from the seaward side of the mangrove forest rose to a peak during Layer 10, and then went into a steady decline. The pattern for the landward side of the mangroves, however, while always based on relatively few species, offered a contrast. Numbers grew gradually with time, reaching a peak between MP3–4. Freshwater species were rare during MP2–3, then rose sharply during MP4 and 5. Land snails made a sudden appearance on the site during MP5 and then continued through to Layer 4 (Fig. 4.2).

On the basis of these changes, Graeme Mason noted successive waves of habitat preferences. The first involved sandy coast and marine species, followed by seaward mangrove, estuarine, freshwater, and finally land species. The site, he concluded, was initially situated on a slight elevation adjacent to an estuary and near an open coast which incorporated clean, sandy areas that favored coral formation. Progradation of the coast, and introduction of turbid estuarine water, led to a reduction in the clean water habitat, the advance of

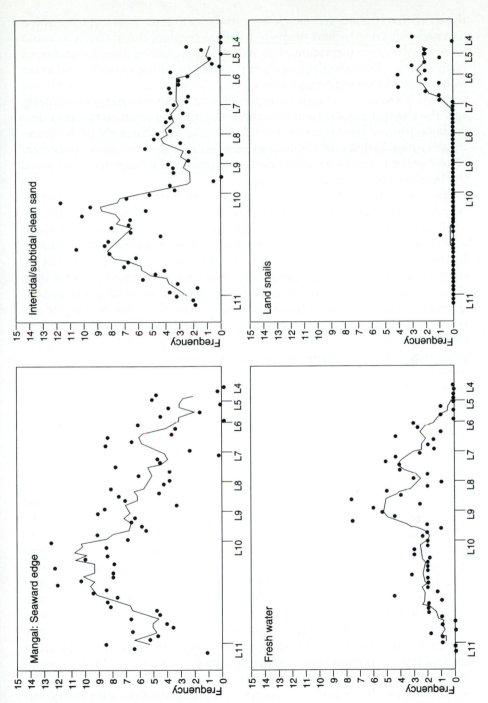

FIGURE 4.2 *The varying presence or absence of shellfish with different habitat preferences during the sequence at Khok Phanom Di. The line is the running mean for four successive contexts and gives the best indication of the chronological trend.*

the shore from the site and increasing proximity to fresh water. The transition to a non-estuarine habitat seems to have taken place during MP4. It could have involved the formation of an oxbow lake, cutting the inhabitants off from easy access to the river, or even the moving of the river channel away from the site following a major flood.

Until Graeme Mason identified evidence for this change, we thought that the site was coastal until the end of the life of the cemetery, and that a reduction in sea level was accompanied by the abandonment of the cemetery. Now we had new evidence, and new issues to ponder, for we noticed at once that the major environmental change preceded the advent of MP5 and the burial of the Princess.

Before returning to the burials, however, results from Jill Thompson's research in Canberra on the plant remains were becoming available. Like the analysis of the shells, there was a long period of detailed laboratory work involving the microscopic examination of hundreds of samples taken from the flotation chamber. The tiny shells had to be extracted and plant remains sorted into charred seeds, fragments of charcoal, and the remains of rice. In order to identify much of this material, Jill had to return to Khok Phanom Di in order to collect modern comparative samples. This also took her to the mangrove swamps to obtain wood from modern trees. One of the problems of studying fragments of rice chaff, the most common form in which the plant survived, is that there are insufficient markers to be sure whether one is dealing with a domestic or a wild variety. Wild rice can grow in profusion in the swamps behind the mangrove fringe, and the inhabitants of Khok Phanom Di could well have collected it without recourse to agriculture.

During this extended period of fieldwork and laboratory sorting, we were looking at a range of other biological samples from the site and wondering how best to proceed with their analysis. These included partially digested food from burial 56. This food was examined very closely under a binocular microscope, and all the fish bones and fish scales were sorted into groups. Who could possibly examine the fish scales for us? We wrote to Barbara West at the British Museum, who put us in touch with Humphrey Greenwood. His report was most illuminating: the person had consumed a fish known as *Anabas testudineus,* the climbing perch. The fish were small, not exceeding 8 centimeters in length. It is a freshwater variety, known to live in ponds, ditches, and rice fields. Small pieces of rice chaff were found in and among the scales, as were stingray teeth. It seems that fish and rice were, then as now, the basis of the diet in this area.

Excrement is an unusual source of dietary information in prehistoric Southeast Asia, because it is rarely encountered. We were, therefore, very surprised and excited when we first recognized samples at Khok Phanom Di. We hoped, of course, that it would be of human origin. Even in the field, we could see that fish bone and pieces of rice husk had passed through the gut. We also began to study these specimens, but it was very difficult due to their extreme hardness. Nevertheless, fish bone, even on occasion shark's teeth, and rice husks were present in virtually all those examined.

We came to the conclusion, from the nature of the bones and size of the specimens, that they probably came from dogs. While knowing that dogs

were able to wander in and out of the cemetery, the lack of evidence for human diet was disappointing. One, however, differed from the rest. It was
much softer, and easier to disaggregate. Under the microscope, it revealed
many fragments of rice husk, as well as hair and much organic material
(Fig. 4.3).

The specimen came from burial 67, and its location suggested a human
origin. Over several days, we excavated it, placing each fragment of rice into
a small gelatine capsule. Without realizing it, we had encountered extremely
unusual and important material, for some of the husks were complete, even
retaining the area where they had been attached to the plant and the tip of
the grain where the awn projects up. The awn is a mechanism for seed dispersal, and it is often absent, or at least truncated, in cultivated varieties.
Complete husks may also be measured, and the results compared with
seeds from known varieties. These precious remains were dispatched to
Canberra for Jill Thompson's attention.

As one of us was taking a turn at the microscope, we noticed a pair of
eyes looking back at us. It was an insect of some sort. How does one identify
an Asian insect in Dunedin? Graeme Mason provided the answer: ring Tony
Harris at the Otago Museum. Half an hour later, we were in the museum, in
a room full of insects of every description. Tony took our sample and put it
under his own microscope. It was a beetle, he said, of the species *Oryzaphilus
surinamensis*. His full report noted that it is a beetle which is often found in

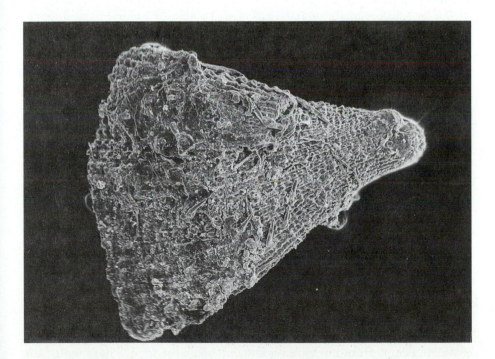

FIGURE 4.3   *The distal end of a rice lemma from the coprolite found in burial 67. The absence of an awn shows that the rice in question was domesticated.*

stored products, such as rice. Perhaps the inhabitants of Khok Phanom Di stored rice surpluses at the end of the wet season for dry season consumption. We also found the remains of a mite and two ants. A second beetle turned up in the food residue from burial 56. This one Tony Harris identified as *Formicomus*, a species that lives off dead plant material, such as the stalks and leaves of the rice plant.

The excrement also supplied us with a sample of hair. Again, we needed help, and turned to Barbara West at the British Museum with a tall order. Could she obtain permission to send us a sample of hair from the pelages of the Thai mammals held in their collection? To our relief and surprise, we had them within the month. At this same juncture, we were approached by a medical student seeking an elective research topic, and she agreed to try to identify the prehistoric hairs against the modern comparative specimens. It seems most probable that the majority come from mice, and the most likely explanation seems to be that the rice stores at Khok Phanom Di attracted rodents. We then turned to the question of human parasites, for human excrement is an important potential source of information on health as well as diet. David Morseth of the University's Anatomy Department volunteered his time, and extracted a helminth egg which is probably from the intestinal fluke *Fasciolopsis buski*. The life cycle of this species involves water plants, water snails, and a mammalian host, usually human beings or pigs. It finds its way into the human digestive tract through the consumption of aquatic plants.

RICE, CULTIVATED OR WILD?

When we began to contemplate excavating Khok Phanom Di, the possibility of tracking down evidence for early rice cultivation was without doubt prominent among our hopes and objectives. We were not alone, nor the first prehistorians, to consider this question in Southeast Asia. Gorman and Solheim were prominent in this field during the late sixties, and the former devised several hypotheses, one of which saw rice coming into domestication in piedmont, interior areas where the runoff from the uplands formed extensive seasonal swamps. Despite fieldwork dedicated to finding the sites, no evidence was forthcoming. Gorman also raised the possibility that the early stages in the domestication of rice took place in low-lying sites now lost to the rising sea (Gorman 1977). We were conscious that the excavation of Khok Phanom Di would be the first in a coastal Thai site that might furnish relevant evidence, particularly in the light of the early radiocarbon dates which had been obtained by Damrongkiadt.

The flotation procedure, under the direction of Jill Thompson, was undertaken with the objective of recovering plant remains, but particularly those of rice. In the event, rice remains were recovered from several sources. The best-preserved came from the food residue already described. There were also fragments of rice chaff in the excrement samples. The clay used in some of the pottery vessels had been tempered with rice chaff before firing, and fragments of rice survived in the archaeological deposits and were recovered during the normal course of excavation. There were also a number of pot-sherds covered on the external surfaces with a thin layer of clay in which a dense concentration of rice husk fragments was present.

Distinguishing between wild and cultivated rice on the basis of such remains is not straightforward. Moreover, it must be recalled that many cultural groups who live in a habitat that includes wild rice do not cultivate it, but prefer to collect it wild. Harlan (1989), for example, has summarized a number of reports originating among explorers in tropical Africa, which describe a widespread practice of harvesting wild rice. In the vicinity of Lake Chad, numerous shallow lakes and swamps sustained wild rice in dense stands. It was a staple for the local inhabitants, who collected it by tapping the seeds into a waiting basket. Returns for wild rice harvesters in the Niger Delta average 600–700 kilograms per hectare. This contrasts with an average yield from cultivated plots in secondary forest in Kalimantan of 752 kilograms per hectare, rising to 1322 kilograms per hectare for rice grown in swampland (Dove 1980). *Zizania palustris* is a swamp grass native to North America with many properties comparable with rice. It has been an important part of the diet among the Indians of Minnesota and Wisconsin, but has been collected from extensive wild stands (Steeves 1952). Indeed, the Menomini, a tribe which is famous for its reliance on wild rice, follow legendary precepts from their ancestral spirits not to cultivate the plant. By beating the grain into their boats, two women can collect between 35–95 kilograms of grain in one day. Wild rice is obtained in a similar manner along the shores of the Tonle Sap in Cambodia (Delvert 1961). These examples are given to stress an important point: the presence of rice in a Southeast Asian prehistoric site does not of itself provide evidence for cultivation. The evidence must come from the characteristics of the plant itself. Yet, because of the fragmentary nature of the surviving prehistoric material from Thailand, hardly any material has been unreservedly assigned to a cultivated variety.

Nevertheless, it is an established fact that, under the selective pressures of cultivation, the rice plant changes its physical structure. This has been demonstrated in an experiment in which the form of rice grown without any human intervention was compared with an identical strain in which the seeds were harvested with a sickle and propagated over a span of five generations. The former retained its wild features: long awns, fewer panicles and seeds, uneven ripening, and rapid seed dispersal (Fig. 4.4). The changes in the cultivated variety were seen in an increased weight and spikelet numbers and a reduction in the rate of seed shedding. This means that the seeds were more likely to remain attached to the plant when harvested, a decided advantage to anyone engaged in sickle harvesting. It is thought to be the result of an unconscious selection of individual plants which have undergone a genetic mutation in favor of a strong bonding between seed and plant. In the wild, this militates against normal seed dispersal, but human intervention by sickle harvesting deliberately selects for it. The awn is a second area liable to change under domestication. In the wild plant, this long bristly projection at the end of the spikelet assists in seed dispersal. But it is no longer of use in the domesticated plant, and it might become shorter with time, or completely disappear. Rice without an awn can only be of a cultivated type.

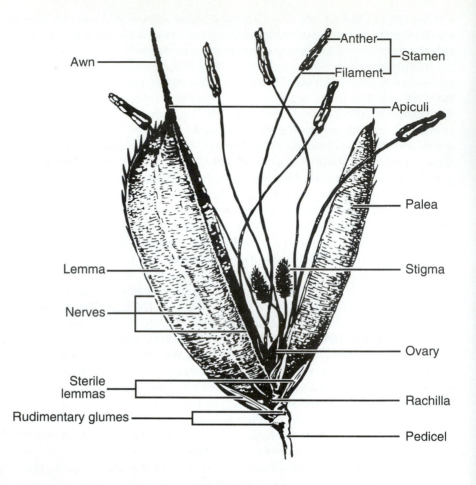

FIGURE 4.4   *Cross-section of a rice spikelet, showing parts mentioned in the text.*

The problem faced by paleobotanists interested in rice is that husk fragments are legion, but the point of attachment and the awn very rarely survive. Much attention has, therefore, been given to the cell structure and
surface patterning of the husk, but without positive conclusions due to their
variability and overlap between known wild and cultivated rice strains. Jill
Thompson has reviewed the extensive literature on the impact of cultivation
on the rice plant, and has applied her findings to the remains from Khok
Phanom Di (Thompson 1992). She has paid particular attention to an area of
the plant vital to its reproduction, the point of attachment of the spikelet
from the pedicel. When this area fractures, the seed detaches and falls to the
ground. In an annual wild rice, it remains there until germination. The point
of attachment must be sufficiently brittle to break when the seed is ripe. On
fracture, a scar is formed, and this is known as the abscission scar. Its shape
varies between wild and domestic rice. In the former, Thompson found that

it is circular, shallow, and has smooth margins. In the latter, it is deeper, with more ragged edges, and tends to rupture unevenly, leaving projecting tissue in the center. The sample of excrement from burial 67 yielded rice remains with 27 abscission scars. Where sufficient material survives for rigorous analysis, they were found to be of the domestic type. This finding has been supported by the analysis of the husks in which the distal end has survived. No awns were present in any of these specimens.

The results of Jill Thompson's research indicate beyond reasonable doubt that the occupants of Khok Phanom Di cultivated rice, but there were many other plant fragments that did not come from rice, and these also attracted her attention. Charcoal, for example, was very abundant in the lower layers of the site. The structure of wood varies between different types of trees, and it was necessary to obtain a wide comparative sample in order to identify the range of species that were taken and burnt at the site. She was able to distinguish between the charcoal from mangrove trees and those which did not come from this coastal tidal habitat. The results were very interesting. Until Layer 9, nearly all the charcoal came from Rhizophoraceae, which are mangrove trees, a position reversed from the end of Layer 8, when most of the charcoal came from other families. The transition took place during MP4, and lends support to Graeme Mason's conclusion that a major environmental change took place at that time.

Several thousand seeds or seed fragments were also extracted by means of the flotation procedure. The most common was an ovoid type with a length of about 1 millimeter, which Jill Thompson ascribed to the species *Sueda maritima.* It was abundant from initial settlement until the end of MP2, when it became very rare or, in most contexts, absent. This species is adapted to open saline flats typically found behind the mangrove belt. It seems that the site was located closer to this habitat during the earlier period of occupation, again indicating changing environmental conditions.

THE BIOLOGICAL REMAINS: CONCLUSIONS

The biological remains illuminate three important issues: the environment, how it changed, and how it was exploited for food. Whether or not the species involved came to the site by accident or human design, they are unanimous in revealing the presence of estuarine conditions, associated with mangrove and freshwater habitats. The proximity of each to the site varied with time as sedimentation increased its distance from the shore. At first, it was clearly close to the open sea in a sheltered estuary. By MP4, however, the sea was further away and the river itself had probably moved away to the west. It was also during MP4–5 that the site was linked to dry land to the extent that it could be colonized by a group of land snails (Fig. 4.2). Only at the end of the life of the cemetery is there evidence for a reorientation of the economy away from marine resources. Nevertheless, freshwater fish became relatively more abundant than those of the estuary and sea by MP4, and the number of shellfish declined at the same juncture. The biological evidence, particularly the shells, indicated a major environmental change between MP3–4. The coast was by then further from the site, and the river channel had moved to the west. We will return to this later.

The Neolithic way of life is usually seen as one in which domestic crops and animals were central to the subsistence economy. This is not the case at Khok Phanom Di. Although rice was cultivated, no domestic animal other than the dog has been identified. This is not surprising given our knowledge of the environment round the site and the wealth of freely-available marine resources. Cattle and pigs were already domesticated in inland sites thought to date to this period, and it is possible that some of the pigs at Khok Phanom Di were domesticated, though there is no evidence for or against this proposition. Pigs were not abundant at the site, and there is no evidence that they were of any significance as food. Indeed, a diet based on rice and fish is attested both in the excrement and the food residues encountered. Even the dogs consumed both. It represents a well-balanced diet and under-wrote the occupation of the site as 20 generations came and went.

5

The Material Culture

◻

Artifacts can inform us about a broad spectrum of activities. Utilitarian tools represent the interface between a community and its environment. How did people employ implements to satisfy their subsistence needs? At the same time, some artifacts may be seen as statements on personal achievement and status, particularly when they are exotic or require special skills to complete. The origin of the raw material of which an artifact is fashioned may inform us on exchange and likely routes involved. Demonstrating local manufacture will inform us how indigenous raw materials were transformed into necessary artifacts for local consumption, or into goods that might be used for exchange.

The excavation of Khok Phanom Di yielded thousands of artifacts. Many were grave offerings, but the majority were either discarded when broken, or lost. The earliest layer included two caches of artifacts, each including stone adze heads, burnishing stones and clay anvils. They appear to have been placed together and never recovered. In the upper layers, we found the remains of a pottery workshop and concentrations of antler, turtle carapace and ivory, as if they had been set aside as sources of raw material for making articles. Broken fishhooks, netweights, and pottery vessels were commonly recovered from the accumulated deposits contemporary with the burials.

Consideration of these materials is a prerequisite to a closer understanding of the community as a whole, and of the changes which occurred within it with the passage of time. In the field, all artifacts other than potsherds, which were far too numerous to be given individual treatment, were recorded to their precise location in the site, and given a unique catalogue number. We found that some artifacts were found in all layers, but others had a restricted distribution in terms of chronology.

FISHING

We have already seen how marine resources contributed significantly to the diet. The most obvious implement representing this activity is the fishhook. Fishhooks were fashioned from one piece of bone. Each had a shank ending with a boss to facilitate the attachment of the line, and a barbed hook. Most had been broken, the weakest point being at the base where the shank began to bend towards the barb (Fig. 5.1). There was little variation in size or shape, although there might have been a larger and a smaller group. Fishhooks were regularly found during Layer 10 and in particular during MP2. They then became increasingly rare. One was found in layers corresponding to MP3, and none during the gap between MP3–4. The last specimen came from a layer corresponding to MP4. This distribution might be the result of an increasing emphasis on the use of this part of the site as a cemetery. But other artifacts, such as shell knives and stone adzes, continued to be found. Another explanation, and one which we favor, is that the actual use of fishhooks became less frequent, or ceased altogether, as a result of the environmental changes involving the increasing isolation of the inhabitants from the sea and the river.

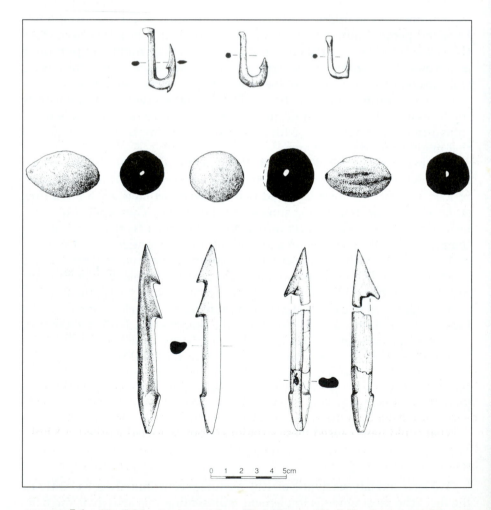

FIGURE 5.1   *The fishing equipment from Khok Phanom Di: fishhooks, net weights, and harpoons.*

If this were the case, then we must also turn to the distribution of netweights. Many roughly shaped and pierced clay artifacts were found, and these have been identified as probably being netweights (Fig. 5.1). They would have been threaded along the base of fishnets to keep them properly positioned. Netweights were common in Layer 10, and continued to be found until Layer 7, that is, toward the end of MP4. Thereafter, no more were found. The chronological distribution is not dissimilar to that for the fish-hooks and might well reflect the same causes. Their disappearance, however, does not imply that fishing then came to an end. We know that there was an increasing emphasis on freshwater species, and these today are commonly caught in bamboo traps. Such traps, of course, do not survive in the archaeological record, but they represent a relatively straightforward and labor-saving technique for fishing which is often associated at present with fishing in rice fields. A final artifact that could well have been used in fishing, particularly for the larger species, is the bone harpoon. Harpoons are very rare at Khok Phanom Di. The specimens have a basal bulbous swelling to facilitate the attachment of the line, and uniserial barbs. Four were found in Layer 10, in contexts equivalent to MP2.

RICE CULTIVATION

In prehistoric sites in the Yangzi Valley, bone spades and stone sickles are often found in association with the remains of rice. It is, however, also possible to cultivate this plant with few artifacts that might survive in archaeological contexts. Swamp rice farming in Kalimantan, for example, relies on little more than a sickle and a basket. If rice is collected by being beaten into a boat, then there might be no need for artifacts specific to this activity at all.

An examination of the bivalve shells as they were being processed on the site revealed that a few bore a concave edge, as a result of deliberate modification (Fig. 5.2). These were set aside for later consideration in the laboratory. My son Tom Higham was then in his last year of study for his honors degree in anthropology, for which a short dissertation is required, and we suggested that he analyze this sample of worked shells (Higham, T.F.G., 1993). He first needed to know what species was used, and Graeme Mason identified them as *Pseudodon inoscularis*, a bivalve adapted to freshwater rivers and streams. When looked at under a microscope, he saw a series of striations and polished areas on the concave surfaces. Some were deep and parallel to each other. Such lines, however, were often partially covered by smaller striations and areas where their surfaces had been smoothed over. Some of these implements had deep concave depressions, while in others the concavity was shallower.

What could have caused these striations? Tom, who had worked at Khok Phanom Di for three months, listed all possible applications for such shell tools. They could have been used for incising designs on pottery, for scaling or gutting fish, peeling yams or taro, cutting the stalks of rice during the harvest or removing the seeds afterwards, cutting meat, hair, or the fabric used in mortuary ritual. It would clearly be necessary to undertake some experiments. Unfortunately, this variety of shell does not occur in New Zealand, so

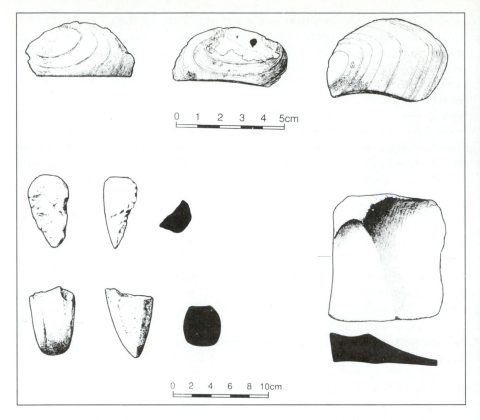

FIGURE 5.2   *Artifacts probably used in rice cultivation and processing: shell reaping knives, hoes, and grinding stones.*

the closest local equivalent, a freshwater mussel (*Hyridella menziesii*) was collected. It was first necessary to account for the deep parallel striations, and these were quickly matched when the initial concave surface was formed by abrading it with sandstone recovered from Khok Phanom Di itself (Fig. 5.2). It is evident that the same procedure was used periodically in order to sharpen the cutting edge.

Each possible use was then replicated in turn. A sample of knives was sent to Alan Grant, then living near Khok Phanom Di, to be used in rice harvesting and processing. At the same time, Tom was himself harvesting wild grasses, stopping at intervals of fifty cuts with each knife so that the long- and short-term impact could be assessed. Brian Vincent then made available a sample of clay from the vicinity of the site, and Tom incised designs on it similar to those found on the prehistoric ceramics. Another knife was used to cut bark cloth, which looked similar to the fabric recovered from some of the burials. A sample of fish was obtained from the University Marine Station, and these were gutted and scaled. Taro was peeled, fresh and cooked meat and hair were cut, and finally a sample of knives was available, each labeled as to its use pattern.

The prehistoric specimens and the modern experimental shells were then prepared for examination under the scanning electron microscope. The depth, orientation, superficial damage to the shell, areas and extent of polish, and extent of use wear across the blade were catalogued for each shell. Some possible uses were eliminated with little difficulty. The shells had clearly not been used to decorate pottery, because the wear pattern was quite different. Gutting fish damaged the working surfaces badly. Cutting bark cloth produced a different pattern altogether. Elimination of most of the alternative uses left one probable candidate, harvesting a grass such as rice. This use produced the same pattern of striations and wear polish, but required regular sharpening to produce an acceptable cutting edge. Here, the experiments at Khok Phanom Di were of less value than hoped, because the knives were used for too long and were never sharpened. Consequently, their surfaces were polished smooth with only a few surviving shallow striations. None of the coarser scratches resulting from the sharpening and forming with sandstone survived. However, the patterns produced with harvesting grasses in New Zealand were available for comparative purposes. We then put Tom to the acid test. Could he identify the use of a range of modern knives which he had not himself used or seen before? We did the harvesting, the pottery decoration, and the taro peeling, then asked Tom to diagnose the resulting wear. He was successful most of the time, and had little difficulty in recognizing the knives used for grass harvesting.

Harvesting knives have a widespread distribution in Southeast Asian sites where rice was important in the diet. In China, many were made from stone, but this commodity was rare at Khok Phanom Di, whereas shell was abundant. The prehistoric inhabitants selected a particular freshwater species for this purpose. The earliest shell knife was found in mid-Layer 10, equivalent to MP2. They were very abundant in Layer 9, during the gap between MP3–4, and continued to be found during MP4.

Only one other artifact that might have been used for cultivating rice was encountered: the large and heavy hoe. Pirapon Pisnupong took the stone implements from the site as the subject for his master's thesis, and identified a series of ground and polished implements far too heavy and blunt to have been used in wood-working. They were fashioned from leucogranite, a stone present about 40 kilometers to the south of the site (Fig. 5.2). Six were found during MP3, three during MP4, one during MP7, and a further three examples in Layers 3 and 4. There is no evidence linking these hoes with rice cultivation. Turning the soil is not a necessary function in swamp rice farming. Hoes might have had an agricultural use, but on the other hand they might have been multipurpose tools, employed in digging house foundations or graves.

POTTERY-MAKING

From first to last, the inhabitants of Khok Phanom Di made pottery vessels. This is not surprising, given the fact that it is located in an area noted to this day for its rich clay deposits. The landscape in the general area is studded with kilns used to fire building-bricks, and there are many claypits surrounding them. Among the earliest features identified at Khok Phanom Di was a cache of 21 white pebbles and a clay anvil (Fig. 5.3). The basal layers also contained many discrete ash lenses which might be the result of firing the pottery vessels.

Clay anvils are still used in Thailand for shaping clay by hand into the desired form of the final pot. They are used in conjunction with a paddle, normally made of wood. The paddle is used to beat the exterior of the clay while the anvil is held inside as a counterweight. Almost two hundred anvils or anvil fragments were found from all layers during the excavation, a small proportion being found as grave offerings. The great majority came from Layers 2–4, when the area excavated served as a pottery workshop. The presence there of a dump of clay, together with cylinders of unfired clay, suggest that the raw materials were brought to the site for forming. The cylinders might represent clay set aside in convenient pieces for shaping into vessels.

While the anvils were easily identifiable, the pebbles were not. It was only when we found them in common association with burials that we began to wonder what they were used for. Rachanie then remembered seeing similar pebbles being used for burnishing pottery in northern Thailand, and this encouraged a more detailed inquiry. Michelle Moore was, at that juncture, looking for a thesis topic to complete her honors degree and volunteered to study these pebbles. About three hundred were found during the excavations, a small number being found as grave goods. Today, these pebbles are used when the clay has been shaped, and is green or leather hard. This means that it has lost most of its moisture and is nearing the firing stage. Repeated

FIGURE 5.3   *This cache of burnishing stones, adzes, and a clay anvil were found at the very base of the cultural deposits.*

stroking of the surface of the clay imparts a sheen or polish. This procedure is known as burnishing. The result can be a mirror-like surface on the clay, which is both attractive and makes the vessel impervious to water.

At Khok Phanom Di, the burnished areas on some vessels were restricted, thus forming patterns against the matte finish of the rest of the pot. Other pots were burnished all over, with bands infilled with impressed marks incised over the surface. Examination of a modern sample of burnishing stones revealed that repeated use on the same area formed working facets, marked by a high gloss and small striations. The potters were reluctant to part with their burnishing stones when asked because it took so long to obtain the desired shiny surface for the best results. Michelle Moore examined all the stones available, and found virtually identical work facets on them, strengthening the supposition that the prehistoric specimens were indeed used for burnishing. Despite the predominance of such burnished vessels in the burial contexts, the great majority of pottery sherds found were finished with cord impressions. This resulted from the use of a paddle wrapped with cordage so that, when it was used to beat the clay, it left an impression of the cords on the vessel surface.

The mortuary vessels are the only significant vehicle that allows us to appreciate the artistic ability of the people of Khok Phanom Di. In our full publication of the site, we have chosen as our logo the view into a funerary vessel from burial 11. This is one of the few complete pots to have survived, and the interior surface of the broad, flaring rim bears a sophisticated and beautiful design, which has been obtained by a combination of burnishing, incision, and impression (Fig. 5.4). The design field was established, after burnishing, by incising two parallel lines round the surface of the rim interior. This area was then divided into two halves by means of two further incised parallel lines. Curved lines of elegance and simplicity were then incised, and part of the field was impressed to allow the remaining burnished area to stand out. The resulting image is of four figures, two looking outward and two inward in opposing harmony. These figures might be simply geometric, or they may represent people. By any standards, they indicate technical skill, mastery of line, and considerable artistic sensibility.

The vessel with our logo is one of many vessels designed with equal skill and in the same tradition that characterize the mortuary pottery from the beginning of the sequence. During the first stage of cluster A (MP2), for example, a female was interred with another rare example of a complete vessel located between her ankles (b. 110). It stood on a low pedestalled base that flared outward to a carination and then upward to provide a broad open area as a vehicle for ornament (Fig. 5.5A). The top and bottom borders are delimited by parallel incised lines filled with rows of impressions. Within these borders lie a series of successively smaller triangles, each in turn being either left burnished, or infilled with impressions. Burial 120 has a pot of similar shape, lying between the ankles of a male in cluster B (Fig. 5.5B). On this occasion, the lower margin of the decorated surface comprises the two parallel lines, but the area has been slightly raised for further emphasis. The design within incorporates a series of curvilinear bands either infilled or left burnished, featuring a central design looking rather like a tied bow.

0   2   4   6   8   10cm

FIGURE 5.4   *A view into the interior of a pottery vessel from burial 11.*

Miniaturization was followed when burying infants. Burial 123, cluster D, during MP2 was only two years of age when interred. Three vessels were placed over the legs, two being elaborately ornamented. One only stood about 5 centimeters high, but was of complex form and exquisitely decorated (Fig. 5.5E). There was a shallow, rounded base leading to a sharp carination below an inward-sloping body and a sharply angled outward-curving rim. Each change of angle incorporated a different means of decoration. The base was impressed overall, the carination introduced a raised section bearing three parallel rows, the outer two being impressed and the inner, burnished. The central area had been burnished to a metallic glow, while the rim section again bore rows of impressed or burnished finish. Adjacent lay an open, footed bowl, the outer surface of which was decorated with successive impressed or burnished rows, the uppermost having a row of triangles which themselves were impressed or burnished in sequence.

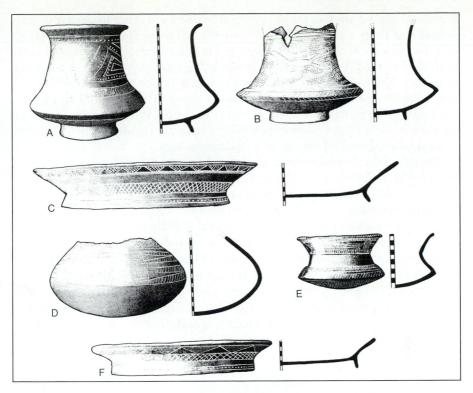

FIGURE 5.5 *Pottery vessels from mortuary phase 2 burials. A: burial 110, B: burial 120; C: burial 113; D: burial 101; E: burial 123; F: burial 102. Scale divisions = 0.5 centimeters.*

A very similar form of vessel, but much larger, was found with burial 102, a female belonging to cluster E. This example also has a row of opposing triangles, but also incorporates a row of cross-hatching (Fig. 5.5F). On moving to the contemporary burials in cluster F, the same open, footed bowl appears in burial 113, another woman this time buried next to a child who died when aged about 6 months. Her bowl had been placed upside down over the knees. There are three bands of decoration interspersed with burnished areas (Fig. 5.5C). The uppermost has the familiar opposed triangles, the next is cross-hatched, and the lowest has impressions. The infant had two highly decorated vessels over the legs, each having rows of curved parallel lines alternating between those bearing impressions and others revealing only the burnished surface. Burial 101 lies just to the north. This infant lived a year longer than burial 99, and was interred with a rounded vessel at the ankles. This pot was not the only one found in which the rim had been removed piece by piece in antiquity. The upper part of the rounded body had been decorated with the now familiar parallel rows of impressed and burnished fields, but in this instance, some terminated lines converged to form a more complex overall design (Fig. 5.5D).

Although some of the forms and motifs found during MP2 continued virtually unchanged into MP3, there were also some new developments.

Burials 90 and 93 are two males, interred beside each other in cluster C. The former had three vessels, the latter two. One of those found with burial 90 was the same form of open bowl with fields of decoration interspersed with burnished bands. Again, we find the opposing triangles and cross-hatching (Fig. 5.6A). But the other four pots herald a form which was to dominate numerically. It is a round-based vessel with a sharp carination and an incurving body flowing into an everted rim (Fig. 5.6B). Without some form of support, it would have been impossible to balance. It is hard not to see this form as one earmarked for use in burial formalities.

Despite their dominance numerically, there are still a few distinct forms. One was found in burial 72, cluster C. This man was also buried with a number of unusual artifacts, including the nautilus shell, a shaped pig's tusk, and a pendant made from the dorsal fin spine of a shark. The pot stood on a low pedestal and had a cylindrical body and slightly everted lip (Fig. 5.6C). There are successive bands of impressions, each delimited with parallel incised lines and interspersed with bands of burnishing. Burial 103 in cluster D, another male, had a small vessel of most unusual form. Above a flat base was a cylindrical body terminating in a plain rim. The horizontal rows of banded fields incorporate a phallus-like motif (Fig. 5.6C). The female in burial 58, cluster F, was interred with a round-based, sharply carinated pot with

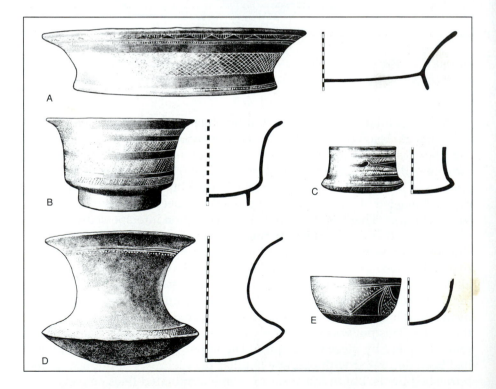

FIGURE 5.6   *Pottery vessels from mortuary phase 3 burials. A: burial 90; B: burial 72; C: burial 103; D: burial 58; E: burial 75. Scale divisions = 0.5 centimeters.*

a flaring, tulip-shaped upper body. Banded impressions are found only just above the carination and below the rim, emphasizing the extensive burnished area between (Fig. 5.6D). Finally, an infant in burial 75, cluster A, had over the ankles a tiny bowl, which had been decorated with alternating burnished and impressed fields in the form of lateen sails (Fig. 5.6E).

Mortuary phase 4 saw further changes. The elaborate decoration became rare, and the round-based carinated bowls predominated. The tradition of decorating with fields of alternating impressed and burnished bands, however, was still alive. Burial 37 contained a child of about 9 years at death. One of the two pots found associated was a round-based form with a carinated body and a tall outward-curving rim. The familiar opposed triangles had been placed above the carination, and the surviving part of the rim incorporated a broad band of incised zig-zags in which the successive bands were left burnished or impressed (Fig. 5.7A).

The regulation round-based bowl continued into MP5, three being found in burial 15, that of the Princess, and four with burial 16. But it was also a time for new forms as vehicles for what we might now call the traditional technique of decoration. One vessel with burial 15 had a shallow pedestal, a rather squat and bulbous base, and an enormously broad, flaring rim. The exterior, where not brightly burnished, was decorated with many sets of parallel

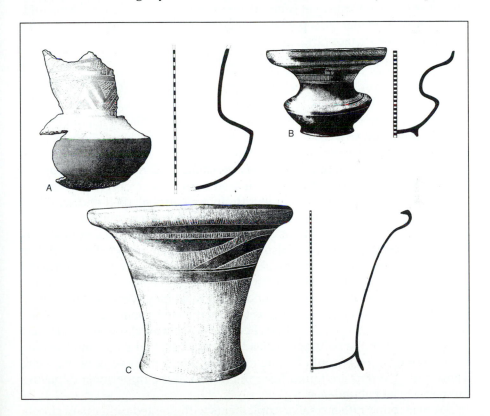

FIGURE 5.7   *Pottery vessels from mortuary phases 4–5 burials. A: burial 37; B: burial 15; C: burial 14. Scale divisions = 0.5 centimeters.*

incised lines highlighted by impressions (Fig. 5.7B). Burial 14 had the two largest vessels found, one of which merits particular mention. Despite its thinness, it stands about 40 centimeters high. The lower part of the cylindrical body is impressed all over; the upper has a series of curvilinear bands between two burnished panels (Fig. 5.7C). As this magnificent vessel was being uncovered, we were paid our daily visit by an entrepreneur on a motorcycle who brought fruit to sell. His arrival, signalled by two blasts on his horn, rapidly emptied the square. My son Tom was early up the ladder, and one of our volunteer helpers from America, her eyes firmly fixed on Tom, asked him to purchase some fruit for her. In slow motion, I saw her ankle turn in a post-mold and her capacious frame descend upon our cherished pot.

During MPs 6–7, the repertoire was again dominated by the small round-based and carinated bowls. The basic decorative technique remained, however, as was seen in the vessel already described from burial 11. It is unfortunate that the artistic creativity of the people of Khok Phanom Di has been preserved only on the surface of pottery vessels, for there are other more ephemeral media which may well also have been used as vehicles for decoration. Fabrics, for example, may have been decorated, and bodies painted. Nevertheless, the ceramics reveal a community that was conservative in the sense that its techniques of decoration remained basically unaltered for five centuries, yet innovative in the creation of new forms and motifs. It is clear that a deep well-spring of tradition and high skill fed the potters of Khok Phanom Di.

WEAVING AND WORKING WITH FABRIC

No remains of woven fabric have been identified at Khok Phanom Di, but the abundant cord-marked pottery and the existence of fish nets documented by the presence of netweights indicates an interest in making and using twine and cordage. An unusual variety of artifact was recognized when the analysis of the material culture commenced in the laboratory: a bone implement about 20–50 millimeters in length with a chisel-shaped end and a U-shaped groove running down one side. It is slightly curved, and the working end was characterized by a gloss resulting from friction with a soft medium, and the edges of the U-groove also bear similar polish marks (Fig. 5.8A). In some cases, there is also a slight waisting on the nonfunctional end, compatible with the securing of a piece of string or twine. These objects are rather enigmatic, and we are not sure beyond doubt what they were used for. However, the most plausible possibility is that they were bobbins, used in weaving cloth. Frequent passage between the warp and the weft would be sufficient to form the polish at the leading, chisel-shaped edge, and the polishing along the edge could be due to the regular compressing of the weft. These bone bobbins are found from the lowest to the uppermost deposits, but never in any abundance.

We also found rather smaller implements with pointed rather than chisel-shaped ends. They too were fashioned from bone, and grooved down one edge (Fig. 5.8B). The pointed end was always polished as if it had been forced

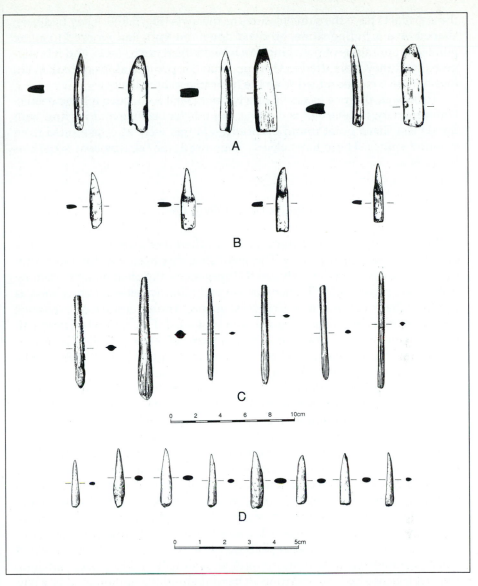

FIGURE 5.8   *Artifacts which may have been used in preparing fabrics or skins. A: bone bobbins; B: large awls; C: stingray spines; D: micro-awls.*

through a soft medium, such as fabric. These instruments have been labeled bone awls, for no serious alternative use could be identified. They were present from the beginning to the end of the site, but were relatively rare.

During the early days at the excavation, we also noted that some small bones might represent artifacts. They were grooved down one side, but their consistent size also posed the possibility that they were fish fin spines. Only when we examined them under a microscope was it clearly apparent that they had been worked and used. Never more then 28.9 millimeters long, these artifacts have the same features as the awls (Fig. 5.8D). They had been shaped on a grinding stone, grooved down one end, and worked to a fine point that bore signs of polishing. We labeled them micro-awls, and it is suggested that they were used in working fabric or perhaps skins or bark cloth. Eighty-nine were found, all from the uppermost three layers.

There was also one example of what may well have been a bone needle. Unfortunately, the eye end is missing, but this tool is long and narrow, with the typical sharp point found on needles. Points were also fashioned from stingray spines. These have clearly been used, for the tips bear striations (Fig. 5.8C).

PERSONAL JEWELRY

From the earliest mortuary phase to the latest, the people of Khok Phanom Di wore shell jewelry. The small shell disc bead was the most common item. We recovered nearly 250,000 specimens, the great majority coming from three graves in MP5. There are several other varieties of shell bead as well, and these follow a chronological sequence. The earliest we called funnel beads, followed by barrel, I-shaped, and H-shaped (Fig. 5.9A–D). These artifacts were often incorporated in the same items of jewelry as the disc beads. The jewelry from the site has been studied in detail by Jacqui Pilditch. She had already completed the analysis of the material from Ban Na Di, then began work on Khok Phanom Di as part of her Ph.D. studies. Unfortunately, although she completed her research on the latter site, she died before being able to finish her dissertation.

During MP2, there were five different ways in which shell beads were used as ornaments. The necklace was the most common, of which there were seventeen. There were also two cases where the disposition of the beads suggested a waistband, and one in which they were found around the wrist as in a bracelet. This was found with burial 133, a 4-month-old infant. The bracelet incorporated five barrel beads of shell and six rare cylindrical bone beads. Burial 113 in cluster F was also unusual. This woman, in addition to her necklace, had a string of beads adhering to the skull, as if she had worn either a headdress or a cap onto which the beads had been stitched. Two burials also had vertical rows of beads behind the pelvis, as if they had been attached to a garment round the waist. The variety of uses for shell beads was greater during MP2 than at any other period, and with the exception of MP5, there were far more beads as well.

During MP3, we found evidence for only one necklace, one waistband, and a bracelet. The necklace, which was associated with a woman (b. 73), comprised four rows of beads. During MP4, bead numbers fell to an all-time low, only one necklace and a bracelet being represented. This all changed, however, with MP5. Three of the graves in this phase had masses of disc and I-shaped beads over and under the chest, distributed row after row in such a manner as to suggest that a garment had been covered in them. The distribution of the I-shaped beads suggested that many necklaces were also worn. Necklaces remained in vogue during MP6, though the I-shaped beads had

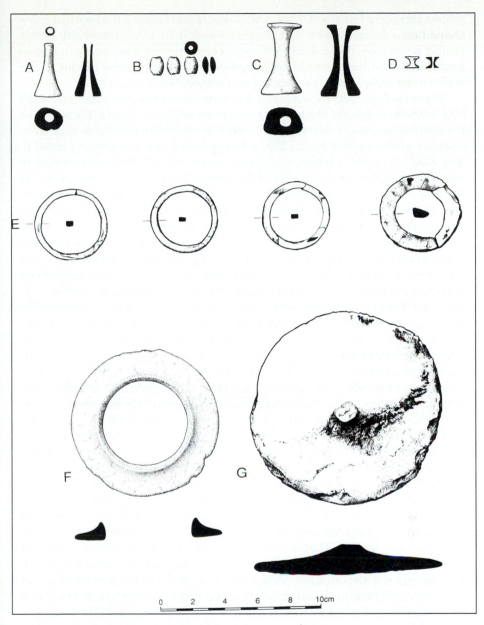

FIGURE 5.9   *Jewelry from Khok Phanom Di. A: funnel beads; B: barrel beads; C: I-shaped beads; D: H-shaped beads; E: fish vertebra bracelets; F: shell bracelet; G: shell disc.*

by now been replaced with the smaller H-shaped variety. One bracelet made up of beads was also found with burial 19 under the mortuary structure. At least one style of waistband reappeared during MP7, along with two bracelets. As with the pottery vessels, the shell beads display continuity in tradition as well as changes in style. It is important to recall that the beads would formerly have had a reflective, nacreous surface that would have shone in the light. A chest and back showing little other than shell beads would have been particularly impressive. Moreover, the larger l-shaped beads are beautifully shaped and translucent. It is not going too far to describe some of the beads as works of art in their own right.

Bracelets from burials were also fashioned from fish vertebrae and shell (Fig. 5.9E–F). Twelve of the former came from MP2, one from MP3, and four from MP6. Seven bracelets made from the vertebrae of a large fish were found over the chest of burial 133, a 4-month-old infant belonging to MP2. In the case of burial 8, which was also an infant of MP2, three were found in a broken condition in the vicinity of the wrists. They may have been worn at the time of burial. The same restriction of a set of such bracelets to the very young persisted into MP6, where four were found in the vicinity of the right wrist of burial 7, a 21-month-old infant. Shell bracelets with burials were restricted to MP5 and later. One was found with burials 14, 16, and 43 respectively during MP5. These were broad and heavy, those from burials 14 and 15 having an almost identical flanged cross section. The specimens from MP6 and 7 were smaller, with a square or slightly rectangular profile. Several such bracelet fragments were also found in non-mortuary contexts. We also noted that, from MP5, a new range of heavy shell ornaments was encountered (Fig. 5.9G). These ornaments were usually made from tridacna, a very large type of bivalve. It is not possible to be sure which species of tridacna is in question, but all likely candidates prefer a clean coralline habitat. Apart from the bracelets, we also find large shell discs and smaller discs which, in the case of burial 15, might represent part of a headdress.

Although the shell discs and bracelets were found with males and females, the turtle carapace ornaments were restricted to the former. The carapace or shell of a large turtle was modified into a cruciform shape, with a hole in the center. In most cases, the ends of the cross members were rounded, but in the case of the specimen from burial 30, a male in his mid-thirties, the lateral ends were fashioned into crescentic finials. As a rule, these items were broken in antiquity and placed over the thighs, to the right of the chest, over the left arm, the legs, and the left chest and hand. The lack of consistency in their location, and the regular breakage, makes it difficult to be sure where or if these artifacts were worn, or how they were displayed. The specimens from burial 24, MP4, had two holes bored at the end of one of the lateral projections, which hints at some form of suspension. We feel it likely that they were worn. They fit neatly over the chest, but David Keightley, a colleague versed in Chinese archaeology, has also suggested that they might have been worn at the front of the waist and symbolize masculinity. This interpretation might well account for the presence of a hole in the center of each. The earliest came from MP3, and all the rest save one were found in MP4 burials. The latest was found in a grave belonging to MP6.

Many stone bracelet fragments were recovered, but the vast majority came from post-mortuary contexts, and none was found with a burial. Several different varieties of stone were used. Three early specimens were fashioned from marble, but most were made from shale, slaty shale or andesite, and volcanic sandstone. The earliest of the black slate specimens was found in Layer 9, but of a total of 63 specimens of this type of stone, fifty came from layers later than the burials. Most of the stone bracelets were found as fragments in occupation layers, the most frequent cross section being in the form of a rectangle.

The same situation was found for the bracelets fashioned from ivory, nearly all the 24 examples post-dating the burials. Some of these were decorated with a series of incised lines, dots, and grooves. We also found a few bracelets made from turtle carapace. These came from Layers 3 and 4, and had a series of pointed projections round the exterior. One piece of turtle carapace from Layer 8 might be a tab taken from the center of such a bracelet during manufacture. A second such tab, this time of shell, was found in Layer 4, and strongly suggests that some such jewelry was locally manufactured.

The inhabitants of this site also bored animal teeth for suspension. The majority were found with burials. Thus burial 15 contained five which came from a small mammal, probably a wild cat of some sort. These may have had special significance, for two similar specimens were found with the contemporary and rich burial 43. Burial 102, MP2, included no fewer than 16 pierced deer teeth. Only after the end of the life of the cemetery did we encounter pierced shark teeth. Two crocodile teeth were found in Layer 10, however, and two teeth from *Rhinoceros sondaicus* were present with burial 120.

We found that 28 fish vertebrae had been modified by drilling a central hole laterally and grinding and smoothing the edges. Only four were found in burials, three from burial 102 and the last from burial 58. There is no suggestion as to whether or not they had been used as ornaments, but the French archaeologist, Henri Mansuy, found similar vertebrae at the Cambodian site of Samrong Sen and suggested that they could have been ornaments placed in a distended and cut ear lobe (Mansuy 1923). The three examples from burial 102 were found near the ankles, but the other, from burial 58, was found near the side of the skull.

STONE ARTIFACTS

Khok Phanom Di was located at a river mouth, and the surrounding plain was made up of marine and riverine deposits. When the site is placed on a map that shows the limit of the brackish water deposits, the broad configuration of an earlier shoreline can be discerned. This would not have been the coast when Khok Phanom Di was settled, because by then the sea had retreated from its highest point. However, it is evident that the site would have had access, either by sea or river, to a hinterland that contained a number of sources of stone. Stone was a resource which was rare, but in demand. Not a fragment of bronze has been found in any of the four archaeological investigations at this site, but there is a range of artifacts in stone. We have already seen that the leucogranite from the hoes was obtained from a southern source. The burnishing pebbles are made of quartzite, which is to be found nearly 50 kilometers to the east. The red ochre used in the mortuary rites comes from shale found near the source of the leucogranite. Other sources may exist, but these are those which are known of in the general area of the Bang Pakong Valley.

One of the most widespread of all artifacts in later prehistoric Southeast Asia was the adzehead. Such implements were hafted at 90 degrees to the handle, and if modern ethnographic experience is any guide, they could have been used for a variety of purposes. Foremost, however, would have been cutting wood. It is not surprising that one of the most common implements cast in bronze, once metal-working was underway, was the socketed axe or adzehead. Pirapon Pisnupong devoted much of his dissertation to the form of the adzeheads, how these came to be modified over time, and where the stone involved could have come from.

Some of the earliest scholarly studies into Southeast Asian prehistory centered on the typology of the adze. Robert Heine-Geldern (1932), for example, divided them into groups on the basis of their shape, and then, convinced that each type represented a particular ethnic group, sought in the distribution of adze types the movement of peoples. Pirapon took a more restricted view of his sample. Had he followed Heine-Geldern, he would have found himself proposing an unusual racial mix at the site, because two major adze forms were found together in a cache at the bottom of the site. Most of the adzes from Khok Phanom Di have an oval cross section and a pointed poll end without any modification in shape to aid in hafting. There are, however, some shouldered adzes with a rectangular cross section, the shoulder being a device to assist in hafting (Fig. 5.10). There are very few stone flakes at the site, which suggests that the adzes probably arrived there in a finished condition. One example, which can hardly have been used in prehistory before being lost, has the characteristic elongated and pointed form and still has a mirror-like polish. But halfway up the implement, the polish suddenly dulls, and it is probably at this point that the mastic covered the upper part of the adze to provide a firm haft. The adze would then have been set and lashed into a wooden sleeve, which would in turn have been wedged into the handle. Without such implements, coping with the clearance of forest trees, boat and housebuilding, or shaping the wooden biers on which the dead were placed would have been difficult indeed.

A microscopic examination of the adzes showed two forms of wear. The first was left during the polishing process, and is found all over the body. The second is seen along and just behind the cutting edge, and here there are striations running at right angles to the blade, which result from using the artifact. Sometimes the blow was too powerful and a flake has been removed from the blade. At regular intervals, the blade had to be resharpened, resulting in striations running at angles to the long axis of the adzehead. Constant sharpening on a whetstone would gradually have shortened the adzehead, and some of those from Khok Phanom Di had been worn literally to stubs. On other occasions, an adze would fracture. It is an index of the value placed on exotic fine-grained stone that broken implements were refashioned and rehafted, to extract more use from them.

As Pirapon proceeded with his research, we faced a hard problem. Precisely what sort of stone was used for these adzes? Fortunately, Douglas Coombs, Professor of Geology at the University of Otago, is an authority on sourcing the likely stone types, and I (CH) rang to ask if he could help. He was the busy head of a large department, but arranged for John Pillidge, one

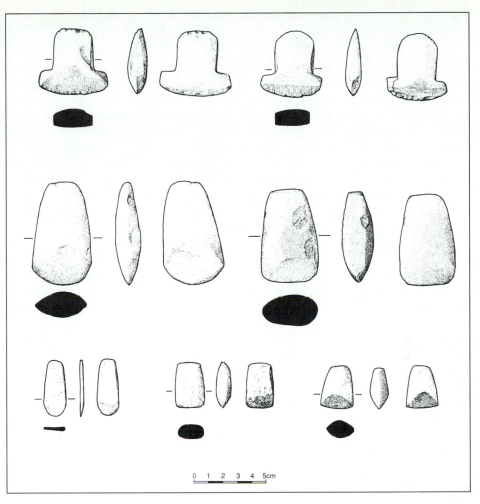

FIGURE 5.10   *Stone adze heads and chisels from Khok Phanom Di.*

of his staff particularly skilled in making thin sections of stone, to prepare
the necessary samples. One afternoon, armed with our samples, we met
with Coombs and he looked at each in turn. As he diagnosed them, we took
notes. It was an afternoon well spent, for we could then refer to our geological maps and confer with Thai colleagues on likely stone sources. This type
of information is commonplace in parts of the world with a long history of
collaborative archaeological research, but it was a pioneering effort for
Southeast Asia. The results were most interesting, for it appears that the
stone quarries must have been located in the uplands to the east of the site.
It is there that the andesite and the volcanic sand- and siltstones outcrop
(Fig. 5.11). One adze was made of calcareous sandstone, and this too is
known about 100 kilometers to the northeast.

    One Sunday afternoon during the excavation, a few of us followed the dirt
roads up into these hills. It is a completely different country compared with
the coastal plain. It seemed probable that specialist adze makers occupied this

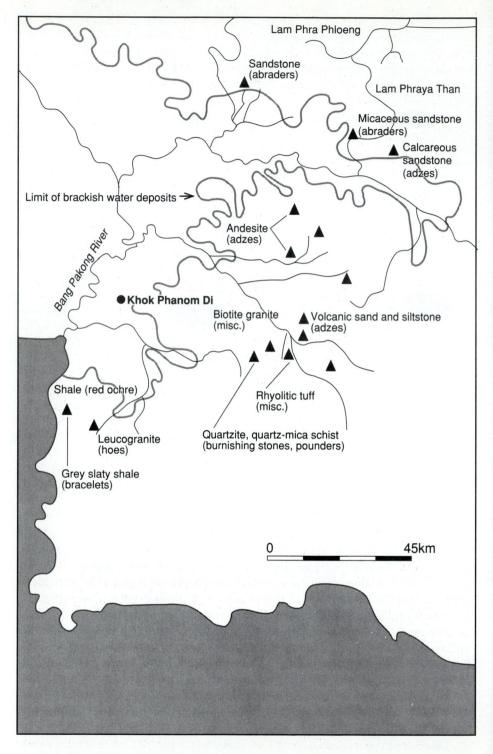

FIGURE 5.11   *The probable sources of some of the stone artifacts recovered at Khok Phanom Di.*

area, and exchanged their finished products with coastal communities. Five years later, when excavating at Nong Nor, we were visited by a local amateur historian who brought with him a pottery vessel that could have come from any of a number of graves at Khok Phanom Di. He told us it was found in a cave up near these stone sources. Perhaps fine ceramics had been exchanged for stone adzeheads.

Some of these adzeheads were small and slender not as a result of constant sharpening but through choice. These, Pirapon labeled chisels, and that seems a very likely use. Naturally, we do not know more precisely what these little tools were used for, because no carved wood has survived. But we might have some hints from a much later context. During the later first millennium B.C. in the Red River Valley and Yunnan Province of China, the prehistoric people cast bronze drums and house models. The former bear scenes of houses and great war canoes. The boats and houses were made of wood that had been ornately carved. It is possible that the chisels from Khok Phanom Di were also used to embellish wooden boats and buildings. This is speculative, but we do know of the meticulous attention given to ornamenting designs on their mortuary pottery.

The ownership of an adze would also have required access to a whetstone. Even such an apparently mundane implement as a sandstone abrader had to be obtained from some considerable distance. The nearest sources of sandstone were about 100 kilometers to the north and northeast. We found many pieces, most having deeply worn grooves resulting from frequent use in sharpening. There were also several large, rounded pieces of quartz-mica schist which Pirapon called pounders. They were clearly abraded on one surface, and could have been used in crushing and preparing food. This stone probably had a source 50 kilometers to southeast of the site.

WIND CHIMES

During the excavation, we found numerous shell artifacts that looked rather like very thin shell bracelets (Fig. 5.12A). One or two had a serrated edge, and we thought that they might be tabs of shell which had been used in making the shell disc beads. As the laboratory analysis of the shells proceeded, we were periodically reminded of these enigmatic objects, and were undecided on what to do about them. One of the great advantages of working in a teaching department is that each year brings good students seeking a research topic. In 1990, it was the turn of my niece Dinah Higham, and she volunteered to try to make some sense of these mystery objects. First she laid them all out on a table, and sought the advice of Graeme Mason as to the shell species involved. He identified them as *Placuna*, a shell still widely used for decorative purposes because of its irridescent surface. None of the artifacts had the form of a complete bracelet, rather they were clearly worked to a semi-lunate form. The soft nature of this shell rules out any industrial use, for they break easily and cannot take a sharp edge. Could they have been used as body ornaments? Possibly, but none had been found in a burial context. Yet a few of the more complete specimens had been pierced as if for suspension.

Dinah was close to describing them as objects of a probably decorative function, when Graeme Mason volunteered a rather unusual possible use. He had seen similar shell objects being used in Northeast Thailand as wind chimes. Suspended in a group under the eaves of a house, they make a pleasantly melodious sound at the slightest breeze. So in default of any better explanation, they became prehistoric wind chimes, and we were left with an image of the mortuary structures at Khok Phanom Di issuing pleasing notes, just as Thai temples with their bell wind chimes do to this day.

SPOKE SHAVES

Another enigmatic sample of shell artifacts comprised tough bivalve shells with deep concave areas worn into a working edge (Fig. 5.12A). No students were available to look at these, so one of us examined them (CH). The species in question were *Anadara* and *Meretrix*. When viewed under a binocular microscope, it was possible to see a combination of thin striations running at right angles to the working edge and areas of polish mixed with worn striations on the outer side of the shell. They had clearly been used repeatedly over a substance in the manner of a spoke shave. Repeated use resulted in a deeper concavity and increased wear on the shell's surface. The most obvious interpretation for these is that they were used in woodworking, perhaps to fashion and straighten wooden artifacts with a diameter of 20 millimeters or less. No projectile points have been found at the site, but the use of traps employing sharp bamboo spears is commonplace in Southeast Asia today.

CLAY PELLETS AND ANTLERS

One of the most widespread types of artifact found in Southeast Asian archaeological sites is the clay pellet. These are round balls of clay, with a diameter of about 20 millimeters. They have been employed within living memory in Northeast Thailand, where they are used as ammunition with a bamboo pellet bow to bring down birds and other small game. They have been found in every layer at Khok Phanom Di.

This frequency contrasts with the distribution of worked antler. The mammalian bones revealed a marked increase in the number of deer when marine resources were no longer immediately available. Working antler into artifacts began only in Layer 4. We do not know exactly what the antler was used for, only that much attention was given to removing suitably sized pieces for later conversion. This was done by grooving right around the tine.

THE MATERIAL CULTURE: SUMMARY

There are many forms of artifacts that indicate continuity virtually throughout the occupation span of Khok Phanom Di. These artifacts include the tools of the potters' trade, anvils, and burnishing stones. Weaving was

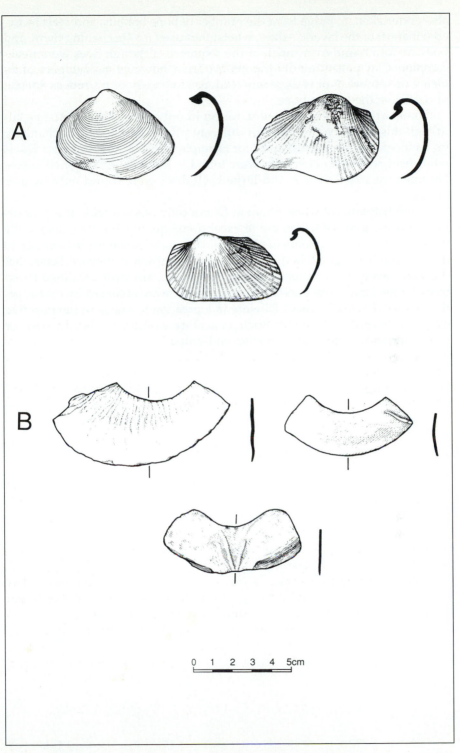

FIGURE 5.12   *Spoke shaves (A) and wind chimes (B) from Khok Phanom Di.*

also undertaken, to judge from the number of bone bobbins and awls recovered in most of the layers. Adzes, whetstones used for sharpening them, and hoes are also found over much of the sequence, although hoes were never common. Clay pellets are ubiquitous. We have, however, no evidence of violence or warfare. Nor is there any evidence for injury or trauma as a result of conflict in the human bone.

Some artifacts were, however, found in only part of the sequence, although this might be the result of different phases of site use, or changing preferences. The very small awls, for example, concentrated in upper levels while fishhooks and netweights were found in lower ones. The shell knives became rare after Layer 7, and large shell discs were found only in later burials.

The inhabitants at Khok Phanom Di not only made a wide range of ceramic forms, some of which are of exceptional quality, but they also made implements and ornaments of shell. All the stone, however, was exotic to the site, and it is argued, in the almost complete absence of stone flakes, that the adzes were obtained ready-made. They were, however, modified to extract the maximum use possible. If stone items were obtained by exchange, the people of Khok Phanom Di were in a position to make and export fine clay vessels and shell jewelry. Such an activity would have been a way for skilled individuals to obtain prestige and status.

6

What Happened at Khok Phanom Di

◻

THE PATTERN EMERGES

Early in 1991, we had begun our first season of excavations at a new site called Nong Nor. I (CH) was heavily involved in the analysis of finds from the first season, but at the same time, finalizing the publication of the second volume of our report on Khok Phanom Di, including Graeme Mason's work on the shells, advising Nancy Tayles on the concluding chapters of her dissertation on the human remains, and corresponding with Jill Thompson on her research in Canberra. I was sitting at my desk one August morning, not thinking specifically about any particular aspect of Khok Phanom Di, when quite suddenly a lot of disparate information seemed to crystallize in my consciousness. I really owe the origins of this consideration to Graeme Mason, for identifying an environmental change between MP3 and 4. I was quite oblivious of this until he had finished his work on the changes in the species of shellfish at the site. Until then, the dip in the wealth of the graves in MP4, followed by the rise to very great quantities of mortuary goods with MP5 had been inexplicable. I wrote at once to Rachanie in Bangkok to sound her opinion.

What I said was this. We must now begin to integrate the many strands of evidence that have come to hand over the last few years. Let us consider what was happening until the change in the environment at the end of MP3. The main channel of the river was close at hand. There were offshore colonies of shellfish species suited to the manufacture of shell jewelry. It was a time when, despite the very high infant mortality and ill health associated with anemia and malaria, men were physically active and robust and some individuals were buried with considerable wealth. Consider, for example, burial 132, a male in his mid-thirties interred with 39,000 shell beads and two burnishing stones. Burial 133 was a 4-month-old child with 17 cowrie shells, seven fish vertebra bracelets and 45 barrel-shaped shell beads. The people made bone fishhooks and netweights. There was an abundance of shell jewelry. They fashioned shell knives for harvesting cultivated rice, and

103

the men had strong upper body strength, particularly on the right side. This is compatible with an activity such as canoeing. It seemed that all these sources of evidence pointed to a community in which men were actively engaged in fishing and obtaining supplies of shell for the manufacture of shell jewelry. The women shaped pots of great beauty and sophistication in decoration. In all probability, given the seasonal pattern of rainfall, pottery manufacture would have been undertaken during the dry season. When the rains come, even today, it is very difficult to maintain continuity in making pots. They do not dry evenly, there is a danger of losing much of your output, the rains make open firing hazardous. So it would have been logical to make pots during the dry season and spend some of the wet season working in the rice fields. It is also evident that shellfish were collected and fabric woven.

No particular social grouping, represented by the burial clusters, shows any evidence for a consistently higher status than another, as might be perceived in the quantity of grave goods and the nature of the burial ritual. Yet some individuals were interred with rather more opulence than others. Why did the women and men have different tooth wear? This was difficult to explain until I read an article by Betty Meehan (1982) on the Gidjingarli people of Arnhem Land. She described how men on specific activities which took them away from the home base regularly, particularly on hunting or collecting expeditions which involved canoeing, would enjoy a different diet from the more sedentary women.

Further food for thought came when I read a number of articles on rice farmers who today live in a similar environment to our perception of the setting of Khok Phanom Di. Apparently such communities in Borneo and Malaysia must realistically expect a disastrous flood every fifty years or so. This might involve major inundation, destruction of fields, and relocation of the river. But the villages concerned, despite such natural vicissitudes, display an extraordinary resilience and continuity. We now think that such a disaster struck Khok Phanom Di at the end of MP3. What happened? The large river which flowed past the site flooded, burst its banks, and found a new channel to the west. By this juncture, the sea was further from the site due to delta formation, and the silty water had eliminated many of the shellfish which had been collected for the manufacture of jewelry.

After this change, we find that the dead were buried with hardly any shell beads. Pottery vessels were less ornately decorated. Men ceased being so active. They were not as robust. During MP4, we find the first hints from the multivariate statistical analyses that men and women were distinguished by different artifacts when buried: anvils with women, turtle carapace ornaments with men. Fishhooks and netweights were no longer manufactured. There were fewer marine and estuarine fish. The teeth reveal a diet that was less abrasive. Shellfish became fewer. There were no longer the deep shell middens associated with the burial area. The number of infants who died at or soon after birth plummeted. How can we explain all these changes? It seemed reasonable to suggest that MP4 was a period when adjustments had to be made to a swift and dramatic environmental change. Let us accept that the river did indeed move to the west, and that the inexorable process of sedimentation meant that the site no longer gave easy access to the sea. The men ceased taking out their boats for estuarine or open sea fishing. The shellfish that provided the raw materials for their barrel and cylinder beads were no longer locally available. The men were not so actively involved in communal activities. In this painful process of adjustment, turtle carapaces were carved to ornate shapes to project masculine values. More infants survived. Perhaps the change in the surface water regime modified the interaction between the mosquito and human groups, reducing the incidence of malarial infection.

While this model of cultural and environmental changes is rooted in the conclusions of a series of detailed studies taken in isolation, prehistorians, when proposing such explanations, must be sure that stringent efforts are made to test, refine, or reject them. How were we to test this set of hypotheses? During all these years, Brian Vincent had been working quietly and steadily on his important analysis of the ceramics from Khok Phanom Di. We had no clear idea where his results would lie, for his research takes much time and we have to wait for his final publication to find out his conclusions. But he had read a paper on his findings to date at a meeting in Seattle in 1989. I fished it out of my filing cabinet and looked at it again. He noted that there had been a change in the source of clay used in making pots between MP3 and 4. A straw in the wind, perhaps, but potters do not try out new clay without good cause. Then I looked again at Jill Thompson's work on the seeds and charcoal. In each case, there was evidence for a major change between MP3 and 4. Again, there was confirmation that something serious had occurred then, at least in terms of the environment.

It is now necessary to try to appreciate some of the circumstances that might have contributed to the dramatic rise in opulence and the change in cemetery planning seen in MP5. There are several issues. Far more energy than hitherto was expended on the burials. They were deeper and longer. The bodies were covered in more red ochre, grave goods increased, and two individuals were buried beneath piles of clay cylinders. A child was interred with a miniature clay anvil. The shell jewelry incorporated a new range of types made of an exotic shell, tridacna. Some the pottery vessels were much larger than before, and bear the hallmark of very considerable skill indeed. The woman in burial 15 also had well-developed wrist muscles. From this point on, women predominated numerically in the cemetery. During the following mortuary phase, we encounter a contrast between three individuals who were interred under a raised structure with considerable mortuary wealth, and a contemporary group buried to the west with few grave goods. It is indeed hard to avoid suggesting that there was a development of status differentials in life that were acknowledged in death rites.

It hardly needs to be stressed that the islands of Southeast Asia, and in particular the recent societies of Melanesia, are a rich source of ethnographic information on the operation of exchange networks involving both inland and marine resources. Further insight into the situation that might have obtained between 2000 and 1500 B.C. on the mainland of Southeast Asia will therefore be considered on the basis of our appreciation of recently documented behavior.

Insight into the exchange of shell valuables in Melanesia is almost synonymous with the early development of social anthropology as a scholarly discipline. Long distance, hazardous ocean voyages to exchange apparently valueless shell ornaments, the *kula,* was an absorbing aspect of the lives of the occupants of the Massim area, the islands to the east of New Guinea. Irwin (1983) has approached the issue of chieftainship in the Trobriand Islands from the point of view of the advantages conferred by a central location. He found that the communities most centrally placed for exchange and communication were those in which members of the highest-ranked lineage resided. This situation might well have had a parallel in the highly advantageous estuarine location of Khok Phanom Di. A further point stressed by Irwin is the scarcity of pottery-making centers, and the distances over which vessels were exchanged within the *kula* area.

Lepowsky (1983) has described the principal elements of exchange in the Louisade archipelago, which lies to the southeast and at the periphery of the classic *kula* islands. It is in this context, and in particular on the island of Sudest, that we encounter behavior which allows insight into the system represented in the Khok Phanom Di cemetery. On Sudest, trading with communities living in neighboring islands is concerned not only with essentials, such as food, but also with ceremonial items, such as pigs, adze blades, pottery vessels, polished pearl shell spoons, hair combs, and shell armbands and bead necklaces. It is central to the system that men and women can aspire to prestige and power through the acquisition and then the gifting of valuables in quantities greater than the norm. In Lepowsky's own words: "Exchange activities in the Sudest area are an avenue to potential wealth, prestige and power open to any woman as well as any man who chooses to exceed the minimal demands of custom in obtaining valuables" (Lepowsky 1983:500).

What were the valuables used for? We find that they were essential in the provision of gifts during memorial feasts for the dead, for brideprice prestations, and in settling disputes. Indeed, exchange voyaging was a means to find appropriate marriage partners among widely dispersed communities. Funerary feasting made a major call on the production of food above subsistence. They could be given over periods of between three and twenty years, depending on the status of the deceased. The economic value of exchanging goods between specialist communities in an ecologically diverse area is obvious. We find specialists in canoe construction, in diving for conus shell, pottery-making, pig-raising, wood-carving, and shell bead manufacture. But for the socially ambitious, success in ceremonial exchange was the road to increased status and power as a big man or a big woman. Nor is this attainment of high status by women restricted to Sudest Island. Battaglia (1983) has noted a similar phenomenon on Sabarl Island on the eastern Calvados chain. The women of this island travel on their own expeditions to exchange ceremonial valuables. She has also stressed the role of the matriline in exchange transactions, and noted how a "strong woman" may advance in status through producing more food than is necessary for subsistence, sponsoring feasts, and showing expertise in the field of ceremonial exchange. Particular stress is given to mortuary feasting, because "Ancestors' graves anchor their memories as well as their supernatural services to their earthly vicinities" (Battaglia 1983:449).

Our understanding of the sequence at Khok Phanom Di at this critical juncture recognizes that the manufacture, exchange, accumulation, and display of material goods are a route to securing status. There are other routes as well. Production of food above subsistence needs, its display, and the provision of feasts, or open destruction may attain the same end. Obtaining slaves and attracting followers is a third route. We know nothing of food surpluses at Khok Phanom Di, although feasting and the provision of food for the dead may well account for the deep middens around grave groups and the digging of pits that contain a high proportion of unopened shellfish. It does, however, seem highly likely that some individuals, at least, were highly skilled at making pots. If some of the grave goods at this site were the property of the dead, then it is suggested that the people who shaped these vessels were women. But who decorated them? During MP2–4, 17 graves contained burnishing stones. Six of these contained males, seven contained females, and children were found in four. From MP5, five of the six graves with burnishing stones contained females, and one an infant. All female graves but one during this same span included clay anvils, the one exception having no fewer than eight burnishing stones. Some of the pottery vessels made were far larger, were superbly decorated and, in the words of Brian Vincent, our specialist ceramicist, could be classified as masterpieces.

These are all observed facts of the mortuary record. They concern an extinct society, and at best we can only offer interpretations based on our own experience and reading of recent human behavior that has been observed and interpreted by specialists. Bearing in mind that prehistoric data such as ours can sustain more than one reasonable interpretation, we begin ours by suggesting that there was a quickening of craft specialization at Khok Phanom Di, which centered on the women. They learned their craft from an early age, if our miniature anvil is a guide. In this part of the history of their community, an environmental change made it more difficult, if not impossible, to obtain good supplies of shell locally for the manufacture of jewelry. This was henceforth obtained from a distance, and it came in finished form. A new range of items was obtained: I-shaped beads, shell discs, and bracelets. By making their pottery masterpieces for exchange, these women could convert skill into high status within their community. Here, our argument could diverge in two directions. It might have been the women who became the entrepreneurs, and their status was obtained by their own devices. Under this situation, the men would indeed have been relegated to a subservient role. Could this explain the poor, headless male interred in a shallow grave alongside burial 15? On the other hand, we must consider burial 43, a splendidly rich male whose ankles, unfortunately, just extended into our excavation square. It could equally have been the case that it was the men who came to manipulate and exploit their women's skill, and whose status visibly swelled as they placed their women, on death, into large graves with many rare and highly prestigious shell ornaments.

In either case, and we cannot judge between them on present evidence, we remain with the basic premise that it was specialization and exchange that provided the means to prestige and status. Our argument that women shaped the pots invites us to try to cross a particularly dangerous minefield. The goal on the other side is inviting, but the chances of injury are high. The issue is this. Anthropology is divided into a number of subdisciplines. Prehistorians are confronted by a mass of material data that make the reconstruction of sub-sistence systems and technology relatively straightforward. But a central and crucial part of any prehistoric society was its kinship system and the rules governing descent and residence. Edmund Leach (1961) identified close links between kinship systems, land, property, and economic activities in Sri Lanka. His work in the Kachin Hills of Burma likewise revealed how different sys-tems of rice farming in hill and lowland settings had intimate links with durable and more changeable forms of social status and control (Leach 1954). At the same time, however, Leach was disdainful over the prospects of pre-historians being able to assess, other than in their imaginations, the nature of prehistoric kinship and residence rules. He called this area of prehistoric be-havior a "black box." One could identify inputs in terms of subsistence and technology, but never understand its contents (Leach 1973).

This does not mean that there have not been a series of attempts. During the early 1960s, for example, Lewis Binford led a group that came to be known as the "New Archaeologists." One of the issues they confronted is highly relevant for Khok Phanom Di. It is the reconstruction of kinship from archaeological remains (Allen and Richardson 1971). One hypothesis was that, where women made and decorated pottery vessels, it should be possi-ble to identify matrilineal descent and residence where successive phases in-corporated the same pottery forms and decorative motifs. This stresses that women would teach their daughters lineage norms, fostering conservatism in the pottery repertoire in a given site. Deetz (1968) followed the same course of reasoning when he suggested that such continuity in the cluster-ing of stylistic variables is a reflection of matrilineal descent and matrilocal residence. Allen and Richardson (1971), in reviewing these early forays into prehistoric kinship structures, issued clear warnings laced with scepticism. They noted, for example, that there is no ethnographic documentation of such ceramic conservatism among pottery-making communities. They counter with the argument that the ideal shapes and styles of decoration may reflect "societal ideals about how designs and shapes should be." They then proceeded to criticise the notion that we can be sure whether it was the males or the females who actually made the artifacts in question. They con-clude with pessimism: "The analysis of descent from the archaeological record in any statistically significant way is an unobtainable luxury."

If we were to agree, and suspend further consideration, we would be left with the nagging feeling that we had not fulfilled our obligation to the data. We had toiled away for so long and spent so much time undertaking routine laboratory analyses that we were not prepared to stop thinking about this site. This perseverance was encouraged by our feeling that the quality of our information was particularly high. It is very unusual, for example, to find such a rapid pace of accumulation in a cemetery that people were interred over each other. Nor does one commonly encounter such consistent evi-dence that females and the young alone were accompanied by the anvils used to shape pottery vessels. This idea finds a measure of support in the ro-bustness of the hand musculature in burial 15, a situation compatible with the regular working of clay. Again, some of the anvils have what look like ownership marks incised on them. Genetically determined features of the skeleton were present in people interred together, or successively within a cluster. But what of the actual characteristics of the pottery? Are there motifs that are confined to a given cluster of burials? The answer to this question is equivocal, and must be considered in conjunction with other aspects of behavior. For example, some of the pottery vessels in graves might be exotic to the site, having been obtained through exchange relationships with members of other communities. Second, a pottery vessel found in a burial of cluster C might represent a mortuary gift from a member of another cluster. There is no reason to expect that all pots within a cluster were made by its members. However, Dianne Hall undertook a detailed analysis of the design motifs on the mortuary vessels in order to illuminate this very issue.

She found, first of all, that there is a considerable element of continuity in the motifs and methods of decoration. Thus, nearly half of the motifs represented in non-burial contexts extended over much of the sequence. However, whereas only 2.3 percent of these sherds have any decoration, 80 percent of all mortuary pots were decorated. At face value, this suggests that pots with decoration were specific to mortuary use. The relationship between decorated vessels and sex, age, or cluster reveals some rather surprising results. It seems that more individual motifs were found with infants than with adults. There are also some interesting results for the incidence of decorated pots in the clusters. Fully half of the cluster F people were interred with decorated vessels, a figure falling to 17.5 percent and 17 percent respectively for clusters C and A. Again, cluster F had decorated vessels in MP2 but cluster C lacked any until MP3. Cluster F also had eight motifs on its vessels never found in other clusters. We also find that the same motif through time was located in a specific part of vessels of the same form.

These results reveal a marked degree of continuity in terms of decorative motifs and their placement. There is also some evidence for different preferences between clusters. These results tend to support the notion that potting skills were a female preserve and that they were passed from one generation to the next. If, indeed, the manufacture of ceramics played an important role in the life of the community as a whole, then surely it would have been a disadvantage if young women left it at marriage. Our evidence is by no means conclusive, but it does support the interpretation that the women buried within clusters C and F were respectively linked by common descent. This would have involved a matrifocal community. During the last seven putative generations of cluster C, there were nine women and no men. The equivalent figures for cluster F are eight women and five men. We cannot explain this absence of men in the former. Were the spouses of these women interred with their natal group elsewhere? Was that always the case, the men in cluster F being brothers of the women, and the females in cluster C just happening not to have had any surviving adult brothers? Whatever reasons there might be, we cannot overlook the fact that women were regularly interred in close conjunction over a long time, and often with considerable wealth. Was descent through the female line increasingly being stressed during these last three mortuary phases? We have identified a number of variables that support this interpretation. But such matrilineal descent groups have to confront a biological problem. A man can sire far more children than a woman can bear. Let us suggest that women at Khok Phanom Di bore up to four or five children on average. This is probably too high, for a significant number of women died in their twenties. At a time of high and sometimes very high infant mortality, failure to bring at least one girl to maturity meant that the descent line reckoned through the female line was dead. We have often speculated that this problem might have been the reason for the end of clusters A, B, and D. If so, it would also help an appreciation of why the death of an infant girl was indeed serious. The degree of seriousness might have a reflection in the splendour of burials 14 and 16.

Summary   During the first three mortuary phases, there is no evidence to suggest that women or men had preferred access to status. Nor did a particular cluster achieve prominence. Men were active, probably spending a lot of time in their boats fishing and securing supplies of local shell for jewelry-making. Women fashioned pots, we think; men may well have assisted in decorating them. Both men and women had to cope with high infant mortality. Infants who survived for a few months before death were buried with a similar range of grave goods as adults, and some were interred with an impressive number of artifacts. Exchange relationships ensured a supply of various types of stone, and many pottery vessels may well have been used in an exchange network. After the passage of about ten generations, there was a swift and damaging change in the environment. In addition to the progressive sedimentation that distanced the settlement from the open sea, the river probably burst its banks and its channel moved away from the settlement. This changing environment saw adjustments in human behavior. The diet changed as fewer shellfish were consumed. Men were no longer involved in securing supplies of high-quality shell. Sea and estuarine fishing declined. Men were less robust and died younger. Women continued with their former activities, but pottery vessels were no longer so richly ornamented. While infant mortality fell quite sharply, there were more child deaths. A ten-year investment in raising a child would therefore have been wasted, at least in terms of ensuring group survival.

Women and men were now distinguished in terms of their burial ritual. Men were interred with richly ornamented turtle carapaces, women with anvils and burnishing stones. We suggest that high-quality pots were now exchanged for, among other items, exotic shell jewelry. Women achieved high status, and there was a stressing of the descent through the female line. Some men may have used womens' skills to their own advantage, but women dominated numerically and in terms of mortuary wealth. Once again, however, status had to be achieved through personal endeavor and skill. The descendents of the very rich woman in burial 15 were interred with very few grave goods.

KHOK PHANOM DI IN ITS REGIONAL SETTING

It is very difficult to identify the reasons why Khok Phanom Di was finally abandoned. However, an appreciation of the long-term prehistoric settlement of the area would certainly help, particularly if we could track more precisely the changes in the environment. Even before the excavation of Khok Phanom Di, we had spent six weeks undertaking a site survey in part of our Bang Pakong Valley study area. One site can tell only a limited amount about prehistoric adaptation in a given region. Human communities usually operate together within a network, exchanging goods, ideas, and people. Villages may be autonomous, all decisions affecting them being determined from within. But a given community might seek, and succeed, in imposing the will of its leaders over other settlements in its orbit. This would represent a major change in political organization, involving central decision making and a settlement hierarchy. We had become accustomed to site surveying, looking for prehistoric activity, in Northeast Thailand. This inland region has never been affected by the sea, and both on the ground and from aerial photographs, it is not difficult to identify the low mounds that so often signal the presence of a prehistoric site. But it was different in the Bang Pakong valley, because the sea had deposited a thick layer of clay. Any prehistoric site dating before this marine transgression at about 6000 B.C. would now lie deep under these clay deposits.

At that time the area was crossed by the lower reaches of large rivers. Lazy and low in the dry season, they are prone to extensive flooding with the rains. Deposits of riverine silt have been laid down, making it difficult to find the sites that might once have been located on former shorelines. Finally, people have been very destructive of prehistoric sites. Where they rise above the general level of the rice fields, sites are often simply planed off and the material used to raise new houses above the flood level. Many of the sites we recorded in 1984 exist now only in the memory of the local inhabitants. On one occasion, we found a site in an unlikely location. There was much cord-marked, clearly prehistoric pottery on the surface of a small mound. Further inquiry revealed that this site was, in fact, fill brought in by the truckload from the actual prehistoric settlement.

Nevertheless, we persevered. Our team of five walked over our chosen survey area about 20 meters apart, looking for the tell-tale signs: a low mound, scatters of pottery, seashells a long way inland. Village names can tell a tale. Ban Kao means "old village," Ban Krabeuang means "potsherd village," and Ban Khi Lek means "ironslag village." Our study area is crisscrossed with canals, and we would follow their course, looking for signs of dredging. The deposits which came up would occasionally include potsherds which could derive from one of those very early, buried sites. One or two sites were easily found: Khok Phanom Di can be seen for miles. Another, best seen on aerial photographs, is the early city of Muang Phra Rot, as it is ringed with wide moats. Probably the best way to find sites, however, is to ask local villagers, or go to the abbots of the various temples whose gleaming roofs form such a feature of the landscape. The local rice farmer will know the land round his village like the back of his hand. On several occasions, we were taken to a remote rice field, and shown scatters of potsherds and marine shell that are the certain signal of prehistoric activity. Most villagers, on finding prehistoric artifacts, would lodge them with the monks in the local temple. In this way the monks become familiar with the location of sites. The abbot of one temple took us out for an entire day, showing us a series of low mounds which he knew in the valley of the Khlong (stream) Luang.

We logged our results and proceeded with the excavation of Khok Phanom Di, knowing that one day we would dust down the file and re-examine it. Early 1989, after Rachanie had finished her Ph.D. thesis and returned to Bangkok, seemed an appropriate moment to plan further field-work. Would we return to Khok Phanom Di, and track the course of those clusters located at the edges of our 1985 square, or start afresh with a new site and new issues? The temptation to return to Khok Phanom Di was al-most, but not quite, irresistible. We decided to try to illuminate a later phase in the human occupation of our chosen study area. A review of our files re-vealed that Ban Bon Noen was a likely candidate. This village name means "village on the mound." We had visited and recorded it in January 1984. The villagers had brought us beads of carnelian, glass, agate, and gold. These ar-ticles indicated settlement towards the end of the first millennium B.C., a pe-riod of particular fascination because it saw the development of chiefly centers, iron-working, and establishment of exchange with distant India. In-dian entrepreneurs sought gold and spices in Southeast Asia, and the pres-ence of their boats off the coast brought new goods and ideas to the local inhabitants.

We were given a permit for three seasons at Ban Bon Noen. Our intention was to examine a particularly intriguing small mound located only a few meters off the main site. The local villagers had told us that it contained burials, and we felt it likely that this would have been the cemetery of the settlement. Both of us feel that the cemetery of a site is a crucial source of in-formation, and we were keen to examine it. But, on arriving to begin our ex-cavation, we found that a bulldozer had preceded us and the cemetery was no more. It had disappeared. Our sense of bitterness at this loss of informa-tion is hard to describe. We laid out a square on the main mound instead, and while the results provided some evidence on the cultural sequence and material culture, it could not possibly match the information that we had hoped to gain from the cemetery mound, which still looked up at us, tanta-lizingly, from our aerial photographs of the site. Towards the end of the ex-cavation, we began to ponder the next two years for which we had a permit for research. Providentially, we were visited by a local antiquary from Phanat Nikhom. He told us of a site nearby that had attracted the attention of villagers. They had found human remains and whole pots.

The following day, he guided us to the site. It was set in the middle of a broad swathe of rice fields. When we reached it, we could see the relic of a low mound, the rest having been planed flat by a bulldozer to make it possi-ble to grow more rice. The villagers had peppered the site with round holes and encountered human remains. A few piles of these littered the site, but we were told that most had been taken to the nearby temple. We straight-ened the edge of one of these holes, and saw about 40 centimeters of soil above a compact layer of shell midden. Most shellfish were from the marine species, *Meretrix lusoria.* Jong, our foreman from Khok Phanom Di, was with us. He has eyes like a hawk, and as he straightened the edge, he picked out a tiny shell disc bead identical to the thousands we had recovered from

Khok Phanom Di. We felt that this site deserved more detailed study, and our eyes turned to the intact part. There, we thought, we would excavate, away from the planed area mutilated by the attentions of the local people.

I (CH) returned to New Zealand to put together the necessary grant proposals. By now, the Ford Foundation had withdrawn from training programs, so it was always going to be a less ambitious affair than Khok Phanom Di. It seemed to both of us that we should concentrate on finding sites that, while contemporary with Khok Phanom Di, were located in less rich habitats and provided evidence for smaller and less opulent sites. It was rather as if, having identified a prehistoric New York, we sought the smaller upstate communities to reconstruct an overall pattern of human settlement of the area. In 1984, the only granting agency to turn down our request to work at Khok Phanom Di had been the National Geographic Society. We decided to try to interest them again. The Center for Field Research was also approached and agreed to include us in their list of expeditions. The Society of Antiquaries of London supported us, and so, too, did the University of Otago. Our proposal centered on a specific theme. We had found a very rich and successful community, which had endured for twenty generations in the same place despite major environmental changes. Towards the end of the sequence, there were outstandingly rich burials that included exotic, prestigious shell artifacts.

What interested us was the overall pattern of settlement, including adaptation to poorer, less central estuarine locations. Could we demonstrate, by finding a site of more modest horizons, the central role of Khok Phanom Di? Was it even possible at this early phase of the prehistoric sequence, that the rich families of Khok Phanom Di exercised political sway over smaller settlements in their orbit? We would need to find a site that was contemporary with Khok Phanom Di, but smaller, poorer in material wealth, and having less access to goods obtained by exchange.

This research program appealed to us. We both itched to be back in the field again, to feel the sense of anticipation as we began to discern a burial pattern. At about the same time that I heard that the National Geographic Society's Committee for Research and Exploration had decided to support our work, I (CH) received a telephone call from Rachanie in Bangkok. The owners of the intact part of Nong Nor had refused us permission to excavate. I had never dreamed that this would happen. Thai people had always welcomed excavation with enthusiasm. It was time for a swift decision. The disturbed area was owned by a different person, who had already agreed to our research. "We will have to open a square as close as possible to the intact area," I said. Rachanie seemed unimpressed, but did not argue.

NONG NOR

In early January 1991, I arrived for another season in Bangkok. We had been invited to attend a small meeting of specialists beside the sea at Hua Hin and spent a memorable week with colleagues in considerable luxury, discussing the "High Bronze Age" in Southeast Asia. Meanwhile Amphan

Kijngam had kindly agreed to put up another protective roof at Nong Nor, lay out the square, and begin taking off the disturbed plowed surface soil. We arrived at the site to a feeling of considerable pessimism. Amphan had identified and cleared out the areas that had been looted by the local villagers. There seemed to be a lot of them. Would this season be another disappointment? Had our luck run out?

We began to clear the whole surface of the excavation area down to the top of the shell midden. Graeme Mason was with us, and confirmed that most of the shells came from *Meretrix*, a species which was also found at Khok Phanom Di, and which lives in sheltered sandy habitats. We imagined that the site had been located down the coast from Khok Phanom Di, and that their occupation periods overlapped. We then began to remove the shell midden and encountered within it a number of human burials that had been disturbed in prehistory. None was complete, but it was clear that they shared the same easterly orientation as at Khok Phanom Di. Towards the southern edge of the square, we were soon through the shell midden, which was only about 15 centimeters thick. We then encountered a yellow soil, the surface of which was very hard and impregnated with fragments of charcoal. This, we felt, was evidence for a burnoff at initial occupation.

A week into our excavation, we welcomed Bill Boyd. He is a geomorphologist and pollen analyst, and his presence meant that we could begin to look seriously at evidence for the environment when the site had been occupied. Bill asked us to dig two meter-wide projections to the square, one to the east and the other to the north. His objective was to find the edges of the site. We proceeded for about 18 or 20 meters in each direction, until the shell layer began to thin and dip, then disappear. This was the first time to our knowledge that the edge of a prehistoric site in Thailand had been found. The great advantage to us was that it was possible for Bill to assess the nature of the natural deposits under, over, and beyond the site. A second benefit was that we found further burials in each of the 1-meter wide projections. One area had sufficient materials to encourage us to open a second excavation square, and so we laid out a 5 by 5 meter area. It proved a wise decision. Nancy Tayles was also in the field with us, and within a week we were finding a group of intact skeletons within the shell midden.

These burials presented a number of similarities as well as differences with Khok Phanom Di. The bodies were oriented with the head to the east, and according to Nancy's provisional findings, males and females were buried beside each other. There were one or two children also associated, but infants were treated quite differently from the Khok Phanom Di practice. We found them in lidded burial jars, two each being located at the feet of women. Although we found a number of the shell disc beads and some which looked similar to the barrel beads, artifacts associated with burials contrasted markedly with what we had found at Khok Phanom Di. The pottery vessels were often painted red. Their forms were quite different. Some of the burials were associated with the familiar burnishing stones, so there were good grounds for concluding that pots were locally made. But some of the artifacts were totally unexpected. We found a range of shell and stone bracelets not seen at Khok Phanom Di. The skull of one burial lay over several carnelian

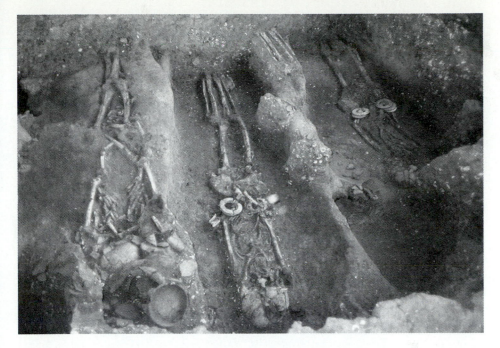

FIGURE 6.1   *At Nong Nor, we found rows of burials similar to those of Khok Phanom Di, oriented with the head to the east, but dating a few centuries later.*

beads. We also found metal bracelets. Most were greenish in color, and clearly made from copper or a copper-based alloy. But two bracelets and an earring were of a gray metal, which we thought would probably turn out to be tin.

As our excavations progressed, so we recognized a pattern. The graves were laid out in a series of six rows (Fig. 6.1). The individuals were interred with a range of pottery vessels, some of which were painted, others plain or bearing incised geometric designs. There was a novel form of shell neck pendant, long and narrow with a hole bored through the long axis. Dog skulls had been placed beyond the human head, and one man wore a heavy shell bracelet on his right wrist. One grave contained the remains of a man who had stood nearly six feet tall. He was buried with eight pottery vessels, a dog's skull, shell disc beads, a shell pendant, a burnishing stone, and a stone bracelet. He was as rich, in terms of grave goods, as all but the very best-endowed people from Khok Phanom Di. Another grave attained a length of 4 meters, even longer than the Princess's grave. It contained the skeleton of a male with a heavy bronze bracelet on one hand and a stone one on the other, several painted pots, a long shell pendant round the neck, and an earring that we took to be made of tin (Fig. 6.2).

In another row, we found that one burial had six bronze, a shell, and a marble bracelet. Another was buried with two bracelets of shell and four of stone. A third, alongside, had three stone and two shell bracelets, a shark's vertebra, and a shell bead belt. Then there were the shell neck-pendants, the dogs' skulls, and the pottery vessels. The graves of this group had clearly

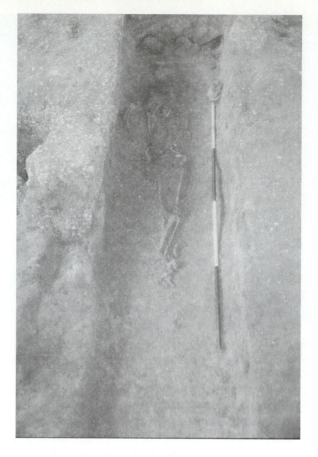

FIGURE 6.2   *Burial 105 at Nong Nor was found in a grave 4 meters long. A male was buried with a bronze and a stone bracelet, many pottery vessels, a shell neck-pendant, and a tin earring.*

been cut through the shell midden. One person had a dozen roundels of shell, which looked as if they had been cut out in making shell bracelets. The twelfth, when we uncovered it and turned it over, proved the point, for it was unfinished, and the bracelet was still partially attached. The adjacent grave had been buried with a huge boar's tusk, two serpentine bracelets, a serpentine belt ornament, many pottery vessels, and a clay anvil. The same row contains only part of a skeleton, but adjacent to the knee we found a group of ten small, socketed bronze implements looking rather like chisels. Beyond lay a further row. Three graves had been superimposed here, the middle one probably having been disturbed with the interment of the first. The skull had been relocated and the limb bones placed in a neat circle round it. Another person had worn a most extraordinary pair of tin bracelets, one on each arm. They were spiraliform, making three circuits round the arm before terminating.

These burials were cut into the shell midden, which itself overlay lenses of red soil rich in charcoal, containing much pottery and clay anvils. The anvils differed from those we had grown familiar with at Khok Phanom Di, since none had a handle. The charcoal was taken for radiocarbon dating, while a sample of charcoal from within an infant's burial jar was also reserved for dating purposes.

While this activity in the square was gathering pace, Bill Boyd was examining the stratigraphy in a series of holes dug around the edges of the site. He encountered layers of riverine alluvium and clay-rich silts that were probably laid down during the period of high sea level. By analyzing these deposits and following their likely course on aerial photographs, he was able to suggest that the site had been located on the edge of a former shoreline characterized by a number of estuaries and semi-enclosed embayments. It was on the western edge of one such embayment that the people of Nong Nor lived. Sheltered from the open shore, they were able to obtain easy access to marine resources.

Our feeling of pessimism during the early days at Nong Nor had by now evaporated. We had recovered 115 graves, some disturbed but many complete, a wide range of material culture, and much information on the habitat of the prehistoric occupants. We had found another site where pots were made, marine food was available, and many goods were obtained by exchange. Although we had found over a million shellfish, however, there were relatively few fishhooks. Many of the artifacts we had recovered at Khok Phanom Di were absent. There were no shell knives, no awls or bobbins, no turtle carapace ornaments.

The first issue to be addressed after the excavation concerned dating. I had returned with six samples of charcoal. My son Tom was working on his doctorate at the University of Waikato's radiocarbon dating laboratory. The necessary forms were duly completed, and the samples were sent to him. We predicted a date between 2000–1000 B.C., although we were uncertain whether the dense shell midden and the burials cut into it were of the same period or represented two different and unrelated episodes.

Tom had to prepare the samples meticulously, for rootlets had penetrated the charcoal, and there was a possible problem with later carbonates being absorbed. Pretreatment to the highest specification was necessary and undertaken. Tom began with one of the samples, and during the period of counting its radioactivity, and therefore its age, I received messages from him reporting progress. It seemed, one said, to be promising. One thing an archaeologist loathes more than almost all else is a series of contradictory and, therefore, largely meaningless dates. I was working on an unrelated subject when my computer indicated the arrival of a new message from Waikato. The first sample was 3670 plus or minus 180 B P., which when converted to the Christian calendar, was slightly earlier than the initial settlement of Khok Phanom Di.

But one swallow doesn't make a summer. There were five more samples to be counted. A fortnight later, the next two came down the computer system: 3910 plus or minus 150 and 3890 plus or minus 180 B.P. A nice, consistent pattern was unfolding. Then the next two ten days later: 3930 plus or minus 90 and 3980 plus or minus 120 B.P. We had a tight group of virtually identical dates, their weighted average after correction being 2459 B.C. The last to come dated the burial pot, and therefore the cemetery phase. It was 2720 B.P., or about 800 B.C.

Unfortunately, we had no other charcoal samples suitable for dating from the cemetery phase at the site, so we turned to a novel way of dating. Oxford University has developed the technique of accelerator mass spectroscopy (AMS) dating, which makes it possible to date very small samples. We submitted five shards of pottery taken from mortuary pots, a source undoubtedly associated with the cemetery phase. Rupert Housely of the Oxford laboratory had already dated some similar samples from Pengtoushan in China, and we hoped that we would receive a set of results similar to that reported from inside the burial pot. Rupert's letter containing the results brought the good news that, indeed, the cemetery belongs to the period of 1200–800 B.C.

Clearly, we had a two-period site. The shell deposits were about five hundred years earlier than Khok Phanom Di, the cemetery about one thousand years later. I quickly informed Rachanie of the news, and by letter over the next few weeks, we discussed the implications. At least in our part of Central Thailand, we had evidence for settlement by 2500 B.C. on the raised shore, but the settlement was not of long duration. Those responsible for the shell midden had chosen to live on a sheltered embayment giving access to rich marine resources. One of our next tasks would be to see if they also grew rice, and for this purpose, we would have to look to see if their pottery was tempered with rice chaff, for none remained in the shell midden itself. They abandoned their site, perhaps due to the silting up of their embayment. These people could have been the sort who had initially founded Khok Phanom Di. No metal of any sort was found at Khok Phanom Di, but by the time the later cemetery of Nong Nor was in use, we find tin and bronze jewelry being worn, and a range of stone far greater than was represented at Khok Phanom Di, including carnelian, jade, talc, serpentine, and marble.

Bill Boyd also noted a most interesting point. The sea level would have been higher at Nong Nor during its shell midden phase than at Khok Phanom Di. Indeed, when Nong Nor was occupied, Khok Phanom Di would still have been under water. This fact suggests a progradation of the land, and possibly a small drop in sea level or isostatic rise in the land surface between their respective occupations. Under these circumstances, we should expect Nong Nor to be rather earlier.

This hypothesis, too, is supported by a consideration of another site in the general area. Khok Phutsaa is a low mound about 4 kilometers west of Nong Nor. A new temple building was constructed there in the early eighties, and Pirapon Pisnupong (1981) directed a small excavation in the affected area. He encountered a shell midden 1.9 meters deep which contained *Anadara* and *Meretrix* shells, the remains of mangrove crabs, rays, and fish, all indicating a coastal habitat during occupation. He also found a row of inhumation graves with the heads pointing to the east, associated with pottery vessels, some of which have similar forms to those found at Khok Phanom Di. There were also bone awls, adzes, and clay anvils all virtually identical with those from Khok Phanom Di, indicating beyond doubt the presence of a similar site about 12 kilometers down the coast from the large estuary. According to its location, Khok Phutsaa would have been occupied after the shore had prograded away from the embayment on which Nong Nor had been located.

Summary   Nong Nor reminded us once again that excavations in this area, where so little is known, cannot be expected to yield the results predicted. Where we had anticipated a small and poor settlement, occupied within part of the Khok Phanom Di sequence, we encountered a two-phase site, which demonstrates the establishment of small coastal communities before Khok Phanom Di, and the introduction of bronze and tin in addition to an impressive list of exotic stone jewelry at a period when Khok Phanom Di had been abandoned.

According to the distribution of marine and brackish water deposits, Nong Nor is located at the very edge of the highest point reached by the sea during the Holocene period. We expect and hope that one day we will encounter prehistoric settlements that will date even earlier than Nong Nor. As yet, however, no such sites have been found. Their current absence has a bearing on the place of Khok Phanom Di on a wider stage, a theme that will now be considered.

7

Khok Phanom Di
in Its Wider Perspective

□

This description of Khok Phanom Di has paid particular attention to the way in which social relationships were ordered, and how they changed with time. It has been stressed that it is impossible to appreciate this central characteristic of human culture without reference to the environment, its potential and its changes, the economy, and the technology of the people, in particular how they used their skill to add value to local resources.

KHOK PHANOM DI AND SEDENTISM

This brings us to a review of the particular characteristics of the environment of this site, and its broad implications. We have seen that the modern name of Khok Phanom Di means "Good Mound." It was equally a good mound for the prehistoric occupants, at least to judge from their staying there over such a long period. This, we feel, was in large measure the result of proximity to an estuary and the associated food resources. Ecologists measure the wealth of an ecosystem by estimating the gross primary productivity in terms of k-calories per square meter per annum. Thus, according to Odum (1971), the marine ecosystem in general covers 72.4 percent of the world's surface, if one excludes icecaps. Of this marine area, the open ocean accounts for just over 90 percent, but produces only 1000 k-calories per square meter per annum. Estuaries and reefs, on the other hand, while accounting for only 0.5 percent of the marine habitat, produce twenty times as much energy. Of the terrestrial ecosystems, only the tropical evergreen forest matches this figure. Yet such rainforests have not been densely settled by human societies, because most productivity is expressed in leafy vegetation, exploited by the bird, insect, and small mammalian species that are adapted to the high canopy. Even in areas under modern, mechanized agricultural regimes, the primary productivity is only 60 percent that of the estuary.

Why should this be so? There are, of course, estuarine habitats wherever there are rivers, but the most productive of all lie in the tropics, particularly where there are mangrove forests in the vicinity. This situation reflects a food chain in which mangrove leaves play a critical role. In the Mabok Forest of Sumatra, 12 tons of mangrove leaves fall on every hectare of the shore, between 40–90 percent of which are consumed within twenty days (Whitten et al. 1984). Heald and Odum (1971) have described a leaf fall of 9 tons per hectare from the mangrove forests of Florida. In southern Thailand, there is no seasonal variation in leaf fall, ensuring a constant, predictable source of food (Christensen and Wium-Anderson 1977). The mudflats which are exposed at low tide in estuarine habitats add to the basic food supply, since they sustain a wide range of higher plant species, diatoms, and algae that feed on them.

Mangrove leaves, as well as estuarine marsh grasses and other plant species, underpin a complex food chain, beginning with the fungi and bacteria that break them down. These are in turn ingested by a range of small detritus feeders, which includes shrimps, small crabs and fish, insect larvae, and bivalve shellfish. From this middle order stage in the food chain, larger species become involved. Macaques are well adapted to the mangrove forests, including crabs in their diet. There are numerous species of birds which prey on the fish and marine invertebrates, while progressively larger carnivorous fish are attracted to the estuary for feeding and spawning. Human communities extract energy from this ecosystem at various levels. Bivalve shellfish are often densely packed, and provide a reliable source of food even if collection and transport can be time-consuming. Russel-Hunter (1970) has stressed that the estuarine bivalves are uniquely adapted to the tides and are usually encountered in great numbers. Fishing is easy, particularly when using nets.

Nor is the supply of food in tropical estuarine habitats entirely aquatic. The mangrove trees themselves are a source of edible leaves and fruits, and their flowers attract bees. Where rivers regularly flood, they may deposit silt to form levees. These levees, raised as they are above the surrounding terrain, attract settlement. They also prevent access to the main channel for small streams, which then form seasonal swamps. Today, and surely during prehistory as well, such swamps encourage the growth of annual grasses, such as rice.

Food resources in abundance could well have attracted prehistoric settlement to Khok Phanom Di, but there are other favorable factors to consider. Communication in Southeast Asia is greatly facilitated by water. From the earliest European contact, river transport was fast, land transport difficult and slow. An estuarine location not only ensured access to and control of the hinterland, but also opened the possibility of coastal and marine movement. This would have been of considerable importance, because the food wealth of the estuarine habitat is often countered by a dearth of raw materials. In the Gulf of Siam area, where four major rivers have their estuaries, good potting clay and certain species of shellfish used in fashioning jewelry might be present, but stone, so essential for a variety of industrial purposes, and copper and tin were invariably absent and could only have been obtained through exchange.

There are also more insidious, longer-term disadvantages for occupants of a tropical estuary, and it is through a long occupation of a site such as Khok Phanom Di that we can see these coming into play. The first reflects the power and unpredictability of the river. Southeast Asia's monsoon climate means that rivers which originate in the eastern Himalayas, such as the Mekong and Yangzi, have their wet season flows augmented by the spring melt of snow. The Chao Phraya and Bang Pakong, which flow into the Gulf of Siam, are shorter but even so carry a considerable load of silt. This results in rapid progradation of the shore, so that an estuarine site will be progressively distanced from the sea. These rivers are also prone to burst their banks periodically with devastating floods. They cross a very flat landscape and form oxbow lakes. Occasionally, they find a new channel, moving away from former riverine settlements. The inhabitants of Khok Phanom Di, therefore, would have faced the likelihood of periodic environmental changes both sudden and potentially catastrophic.

In order to appreciate the relationships that may develop between prehistoric communities and a rich coastal habitat, it is necessary to look briefly beyond the confines of Southeast Asia. Two areas in particular are useful: Japan and the western seaboard of America, from California to Alaska. These groups counter a widely held myth that hunter-gatherer communities are necessarily mobile, concerned daily with obtaining food, and simple in terms of social organization. On the contrary, many of them were more complex socially than a good number of agricultural communities. The basic point is that the marine habitat is sufficiently rich and predictable in terms of food resources to enable communities to become sedentary.

A sedentary community is one in which its members choose to live permanently in one place. Such groups, whether they rely on agriculture or not, have the potential to become more complex in many ways: technical, social, and in terms of subsistence. In East Asia, this is best documented in the case of the prehistoric Jomon people of Japan. The establishment of a coast indented with numerous bays and estuaries meant that there were sufficient food resources to permit the establishment of sedentary communities. In terms of technology, this allowed for experimentation and the development of a new range of artifacts. Foremost of these was pottery. The conversion of a plastic medium, clay, into a virtually indestructable range of containers through the application of heat represents a major technological achievement. Although ceramic wares are durable, they are also fragile. A mobile hunter-gatherer would be better equipped with a flexible leather or fabric container, than one liable to fracture if dropped. Pottery was first employed among the Jomon people of Japan, in a growing number of sedentary, coastal sites. Sedentism also nourished the human propensity to ascribe special qualities to material. The ownership of a Mercedes car, or a diamond tiara, is a message of status. A house provides more than shelter, its location and size can be employed to reflect social attainment. Among sedentary prehistoric people, the same messages can be recognized, although at times they are muted or confusing. One of the advantages to the prehistorian when attempting to receive these signals, is that it is possible to identify whether some objects were of local or exotic origin. Ornaments made of an exotic substance, for example, are likely to have been emblems of personal status or achievement on account of their intrinsic rarity. Again, while simple cooking pots may have been of little use in signaling high status, the ownership of exotic vessels, or those requiring a high level of skill to manufacture, could be used in this way.

An advantage of sedentism found in Jomon and many other such coastal groups is that people are to be found in a predictable place, and through the medium of water transport, can be reached. This is an encouragement to the production and exchange of goods symbolizing achievement. In life, this may be expressed through display, ownership, or even public gift giving or the ritual destruction of rarities. With death, it can be seen in the interment of the burial offerings, and the expenditure of energy in providing an impressive tomb, or a series of opulent mortuary feasts.

Sedentism removes the need to carry one's possessions between temporary encampments, and therefore permits the accumulation of often weighty belongings. Mobile hunter-gatherers have to transport young children. Until a child reaches an age when it can walk at the same pace as adults, it must be carried, unless the group moves by boat. This is a strong incentive to space births. Sedentism removes this constraint, and therefore makes possible a more rapid growth in population. As a social group grows in numbers, it reaches population thresholds which can be stressful, for while a group of three of four families might well make communal decisions by consensus, twenty families probably will not. Communication problems and the likelihood of disagreement increase with numbers. There are ways of mediating this situation. One is quite simply for a segment of the group to vote with its feet and establish a new, smaller village. A second is to invest an individual with authority in decision making. One route leads to an increase in the number of settlements, another the establishment of social ranking. Both are a reflection of a growing population. Our review of prehistoric agricultural communities in Southeast Asia has revealed a number of common characteristics. We find that the village, seldom covering more than a few hectares, was a widespread form of settlement. The inhabitants seem to have been divided by status differentials, usually expressed in mortuary practices within inhumation cemeteries. There is some evidence for craft specialization and a propensity for population growth and the expansion of settlement, particularly in suitable low-lying wetlands.

Artifacts, whether they be the particular qualities of a pottery vessel or ornaments fashioned from exotic materials, are but one way of expressing in a physical way the status of individuals. Another is the provision of food. The twentieth-century observer could be forgiven for assuming that food is and has always been scarce. The tropical estuary is one habitat where a food shortage is virtually inconceivable. Food can be used to obtain and indeed measure relative status in several ways. The first lies in its accumulation and gifting in feasts. To give is to establish indebtedness. Full reciprocity indicates equal capacity to give. Anything less is an expression of social inferiority. Rare or exotic food adds a new dimension to the equation. The accumulation of a surplus to exchange opens a route to higher wealth and status. One way of obtaining such a surplus is to grow more through the encouragement of a particular species at the expense of its competitors. Rice, for example, is in nature an insignificant swamp grass. If people invest their effort in expanding its natural habitat and choose favorable varieties for seeding, surpluses can be diverted to achieve social objectives.

Sedentary communities, particularly where they have not developed techniques for agriculture or the domestication of animals, must choose where they live carefully in order to ensure the food supply throughout the year. Few habitats are not seasonal in one way or another, and changing seasons usually involve the ebb and flow of food sources. Occupation of a site for longer than a generation will confront a group with the problem of the disposal of the dead. A mobile group is unlikely to have a permanent cemetery, but a sedentary society may. As with food and artifacts, we often find that a cemetery becomes a social statement. In the first place, the presence of the ancestors in the ground is the equivalent in literate societies of a deed of its ownership. But it is the living who dispose of the dead, and the manner in which they undertake this is a rich source of information. The energy expended in raising a monument, digging a hole, providing a receptacle for the dead, provisioning a mortuary feast, or burying valuable goods, all these leave evidence for assessing the group as a whole.

Sedentism opens many possible routes to increased size and complexity of human societies, but these are not necessarily taken. When we visit the archaeological evidence for adaptation to the new coastal conditions in East and Southeast Asia and Australia, we encounter quite different patterns which are, at least in part, a result of spiritual values which affect attitudes to the environment. In Jomon Japan, for example, we encounter villages in which social distinctions became sharply defined with time, where exotic goods were exchanged, summer food surpluses were stored, and where cemeteries were established in which hierarchies are evident. Yet no convincing evidence has been adduced for the widespread adoption of agriculture. Changing sea levels and a reduction in the natural food resources involved depopulation of the Kanto Plain in the late Jomon period, and indeed, it was following the introduction of rice as an exotic cultivated cereal that we encounter the growth in cultural complexity that characterized the Yayoi culture.

There is, however, no predetermined path for coastal communities to follow. In northern Australia, where river estuaries and their hinterlands provide a steady supply of food, including wild rice, there has been no establishment of large, sedentary, and complex social groupings. Jones and Meehan have lived and worked with the Gidjingarli people of the Blyth River, noting how they choose to move their settlements seasonally. They know of rice, and collect it sporadically, but show no interest in cultivating it. Indeed, agriculture would run counter to their traditional conception of their place in the environment. As Jones and Meehan have themselves written, "Their religious system was the key to their world view, which linked them to their land. . . . Above all, it acted as a reinforcer of traditional values and as a sanction against innovation or disturbance of the natural or social order " (Jones and Meehan 1989:132).

The Gidjingarli habitat is very similar in terms of climate, vegetation, and natural resources to that which has been reconstructed for the Gulf of Siam following the Holocene rise in sea level. Yet the pattern of human adaptation was quite different on the Asian mainland. In examining the latter, we may learn not only how a sedentary community coped with the potential and the problems presented by its surroundings, we can also begin to appreciate the profound importance of the human view and interpretation of those surroundings, and how infinitely variable this can be.

Some sedentary fisher-hunter-collector communities of the Pacific coast of North America survived into the period when ethnographers were able to learn more about them. They encountered a complex social system, involving hereditary chiefs, commoners, and slaves. Different groups displayed their own forms of kinship, some being matrilineal, others patrilineal. Status and rank were of consuming concern, and through the potlach system, which saw feasts and ritual destruction of food and valued goods, variations in achievement could be expressed. The complex nature of these communities as witnessed in the late nineteenth century has tended to divert prehistorians from considering the archaeological record of how, when and why these groups developed in the way they did. This situation has recently been addressed, and some interpretations highly relevant to our own consideration of similar complexity in Southeast Asia have been proposed.

Perhaps the most intriguing case study from the Pacific coast concerns the Chumash of the Santa Barbara Channel. Arnold (1991) has noted how early explorers in this part of California were impressed by the intensive concern for valuables, such as shell beads and exchange in products made by craft specialists. This practice required sophisticated boats, because exchange involved both mainland and offshore island people. By this contact period, there were regional chiefdoms with authority over both sections of the mainland coast and groups of islands. Chiefs practised polygyny and controlled guilds of specialists. Arnold has traced the origins of such complexity to the period between 1200–1300 A.D. The subsistence of these people was based, in order of importance, on fish, shellfish, sea mammals, seeds, acorns, fruits, berries, and bulbs and the fox, deer, and dog. The environment, while beneficent, was also unpredictable, largely because of climatic vagaries. The El Niño, in particular, involved a warming phase of currents which severely affects fisheries, since it reduces the quantity of available nutrients. Evidently the El Niño, which manifested itself in the early 1980s, led to a 90 percent reduction in kelp and an 80 percent decline in fish stocks. According to the available palaeoenvironmental data, there was a similar reduction seven centuries ago. Sea surface temperatures rose, fish stocks fell, and villages were abandoned. Human health deteriorated. The newly established villages may have been overcrowded, and water quality probably declined dangerously.

These new settlements, however, involved an innovation. There was a dramatic increase in craft specialization. Shell bead manufacture was intensified; there was even a trend to the use of shell beads as a form of currency. These beads were exchanged from the islands where they were made, to the mainland, where some were placed in burials as symbols of rank. The important source of chert on Santa Cruz Island was also the focus of specialized production of microliths, a trend reinforced by restricted access to the valued stone. In terms of the mortuary data for these groups, there is evidence that high social status was the perquisite of particular lineages, and was transferred through the generations.

Arnold (1991) has suggested that the keys to understanding this social change lie first in establishing the advent of drastic environmental change and its associated social stress. This involved increasing political opportunism by emerging lineage heads, and their control over specialist labor. By controlling two vital resources, shell and stone, and organizing the labor to convert these into goods for exchange, the leaders could exchange local valuables for mainland supplies of food. Parallels between this interpretation and the social changes identified at Khok Phanom Di are particularly intriguing.

The course towards such social complexity was neither even nor contemporary along the extensive coastal tract from California to Alaska, but a number of common features have been identified by workers in different areas. Thus, Maschner (1991), has identified these trends by 500 A.D. in southern coastal Alaska, where large coastal villages were increasingly established with defense in mind, the bow and arrow was introduced, and individuals began to wield political control. He has suggested four factors which influenced this new situation. The first requirement is a steady and predictable food supply, which enables groups to become sedentary. The next step is for populations to grow in size, for the larger the community, the more it is necessary to institutionalize authority in a few particular individuals. These people, he suggests, are most likely to come from the largest kin group or lineage. Valued resources must have a restricted distribution, so that communities are pulled to them and seek to regulate access. Finally, if populations grow to the point that it is not feasible for splinter groups to leave and form new communities, then the ingredients which encourage social hierarchies are in place.

THE SOCIAL ARCHAEOLOGY OF KHOK PHANOM DI
AND CONTEMPORARY SITES

Before the excavation of Khok Phanom Di, several major contributions to the assessment of prehistoric social organization in sites within its orbit were available. MacDonald (1978), for example, has proposed an interpretation of the Ban Kao mortuary data which differed markedly from that offered by the excavator (Sørensen and Hatting, 1967). This is a cemetery located about 200 kilometers to the west of Khok Phanom Di and occupied at the same period. Bayard (1984) then offered a social interpretation of the Non Nok Tha cemetery, which is also second millennium B.C., and Higham and Kijngam (1984) did the same for Ban Na Di, which is slightly later. Both these sites are located in Northeast Thailand, and evidence bronze casting. Ho (1984) has commented on the burial remains from Khok Charoen, which, like Khok Phanom Di, has no evidence of metallurgy but an abundance of pottery vessels and shell and stone jewelry associated with the burials. This cemetery is found 250 kilometers to the north of Khok Phanom Di and, again, was probably in use during the second millennium B.C.

MacDonald has considered the distribution of the Ban Kao burials in terms of several alternative hypotheses, including temporal and age, or sex-based distinctions between different graves. Having found little pattern in these alternatives, he considered the orientation of the graves, having noted that, while some have the head pointing to the east, others have an orientation to the north. He suggested that the most plausible interpretation is that the two groups represent two wards of the same community. This pattern of subdivision, he noted, is not unusual in modern villages in Southeast Asia. If this is the case, then it contrasts markedly with Bayard's views on the social organization responsible for the Non Nok Tha cemetery. In his review of Non Nok Tha, Bayard stressed the presence of two pot forms which have a mutually complementary distribution in the burials. From this, and the different degrees of wealth between the graves associated with each form, he proposed that the cemetery was used by members of two distinctive, probably land-holding, affiliated groups. This situation, following his view of the site's chronology, would have lasted for at least one and possibly two millennia. Whereas MacDonald has his two groups set apart from each other spatially, Bayard has proposed social groups that were buried without spatial segregation over a period of centuries, possibly millennia.

We have taken issue with Bayard's interpretation on several counts (Thosarat 1989). In the first place, the two pot forms do not present a complementary distribution. Some graves have examples of both. Second, we have followed up the alleged long-term use of the cemetery by plotting the graves assigned by Bayard to successive phases of burials (Fig. 7.1). Having first plotted the distribution of graves for each phase separately, we then combined them in a single distribution (Fig. 7.2). It was found that graves which, according to Bayard's proposed chronology would have been separated in time by centuries, were placed in an orderly manner beside each other. When viewed in conjunction, the graves are seen to fall into at least two rows. Therefore, we have proposed that the cemetery was in use for only a limited span, perhaps in the order of a few centuries, by members of a series of social groups, perhaps households, who were buried in proximity to each other.

The stratigraphic and chronological difficulties experienced at Non Nok Tha make it impossible at present to decide between these alternatives, but the issue does reveal the wide divergence of views on prehistoric social organization in Southeast Asia. On the one hand, Bayard's view implies an extraordinary stability of population and styles of material culture. The adoption of bronze, while having an impact, in his view, on the degree of social ranking, would have taken place very slowly. Our alternative view on the chronology envisages much more rapid social change, with the layout of the graves being related to social organization rather than being fortuitous and random. On one point, however, there can only be agreement. It is the importance of opening an extensive area in order to obtain data on the spatial layout of the cemetery. This was not undertaken at Ban Chiang, for

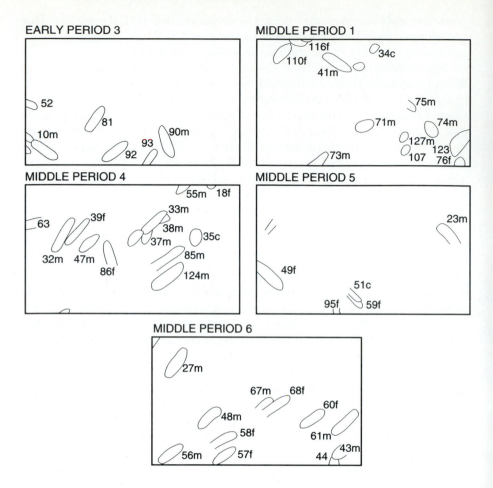

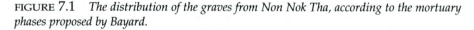

FIGURE 7.1   *The distribution of the graves from Non Nok Tha, according to the mortuary phases proposed by Bayard.*

be ascertained.

At Ban Na Di, the configuration of the excavated area was long and narrow, because it had to fit between modern houses (Higham and Kijngam 1984). However, the excavators had the good fortune to encounter a nucleated cluster of graves in the main area investigated, together with a second about 30 meters away in a second square. The latter contained numerous burials placed beside and over each other, but were found in only a third of the square. It is apparent that the investigators encountered the edge of a cluster of graves. Their social interpretation rests on the finding that the two clusters of graves, while separated by 30 meters, were contemporary.

When the artifacts associated with the graves were considered, with particular reference to exotic against local origin, it was found that the graves in one cluster were consistently richer than those in the other. Higham and Kijngam (1984), for example, have noted that over 90 percent of the disc beads, all the imported trochus shell armbands, all the clay figurines of men and ani-

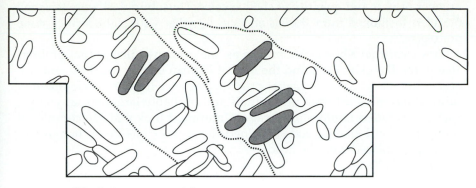

Stippled graves are rich

FIGURE 7.2   *The distribution of the graves from Non Nok Tha, combining those from Bayard's proposed phases*

mals, all the exotic stone bracelets, the majority of the bronze items, and the
first and only objects of iron were found in the richer of the two clusters.
From these data, the excavators have suggested that there were at least two
social groups, each probably comprising related individuals. If we can
equate the ownership of exotic objects with rank, then members of one of
these groups had consistently higher status.

Khok Charoen is located near the right bank of the Pasak River on the
eastern edge of the Central Plain of Thailand. Like Khok Phanom Di, it has
not produced any evidence for bronze. Two dates suggest occupation within
a range of 1480–780 B.C., but these seem too late. Four seasons of excavations
were undertaken there, and the material from the first and second seasons
has been studied by Ho (1984). Twenty 4 by 4 meter squares and three smaller
test squares were opened, providing evidence for the spatial distribution of
graves. The stratigraphy barely exceeded a meter in depth, and two major
layers were identified, the later corresponding to the cemetery phase. Forty-
four burials and two jar deposits were recovered, and it was largely on the
basis of body orientation that Ho subdivided the sample into three mortuary
phases. As at Khok Phanom Di, there was a range of grave goods, including
whole pottery vessels, stone adze heads, shell jewelry including beads, discs,
and bracelets, and the bones of a range of animals. Since some ornaments
were made of marine shell, there is clear evidence for exchange with the occupants of such coastal communities as Khok Phanom Di. Indeed, one disc,
probably part of a headdress found in burial 19, was virtually identical with
those recovered from burial 15 at Khok Phanom Di.

Ho regarded the distribution of the graves and their orientation more
from the point of view of establishing a sequence than identifying possible
socially significant clusters. Nor have the human remains been identified as
to sex. However, it is clear from her analysis that there was a disparity in
the range of grave goods with individual interments, some people being
buried with none, others with a relatively rich set of goods, expressed as the
number of pots and quantity of shell jewelry. Thus, burial 24 wore ten shell

number of pots and quantity of shell jewelry. Thus, burial 24 wore ten shell bracelets fashioned from *Trochus niloticus* together with eight further stone bracelets.

It is clear that Khok Phanom Di was one of many villages that proliferated in the Bangkok Plain and the Khorat Plateau during the third and second millennia B.C. These villages provide evidence for the development of status differences between individuals and probably larger social groups, such as extended families or lineages. Interment took place in communal cemeteries, and exotic goods obtained through extensive exchange networks were placed with the dead.

8

Archaeology, Human Biology, and Linguistics in Southeast Asia

□

When looking further afield to consider the broader significance of this site, we shall call on three sources of data: archaeology, linguistics, and human biology. All fields are moving rapidly, and any overview is only a snapshot due for early modification.

The first issue involves the people. Traditionally, relationships between prehistoric populations have been considered on the basis of surviving skeletal material. This provides evidence for stature, the shape of the cranium, structure of the teeth, and variations in the presence or absence of certain small bones or bone configurations, particularly in the skull. Turner (1987), for example, has considered the shape, structure, and size of the teeth of modern and prehistoric people from East and Southeast Asia and recognized two major groups: Sinodont and Sundadont. The former is found in northeastern, the latter in southeastern Asia. Sundadonts have weaker development of shovel-shaped incisors and higher frequencies of molars with only four cusps. Sundadonts have a higher incidence of two-rooted upper first and lower second molars. Turner feels that the southern group has the more conservative, less specialized dentition. Moreover, modern Thais have teeth closer to the local prehistoric people than to the northern Sinodonts. Thus, there are no grounds for proposing any form of population movement into Southeast Asia from the north, where tooth forms are both quite distinct and more specialized.

Pietrusewsky (1984) has compared modern and prehistoric crania from Southeast Asia with populations from other parts of Asia and the Pacific. These involve dimensions and nonmetric variables. On the basis of 13 measurements, for example, he has found that the people of prehistoric Ban Chiang are very similar to those from Vietnamese sites, while the Non Nok Tha sample closely resembles that for Ban Kao in Central Thailand. He has not yet had the opportunity to incorporate the material from Khok Phanom Di into his results. There are also close similarities between modern Cambodian, Vietnamese, and Indonesian people and the prehistoric groups from Thailand.

This similarity is most interesting, because it is clear that the present inhabitants of Indonesia, coastal Malaysia, Thailand, Vietnam, and southern China, and the inhabitants of Polynesia are racially southern Mongoloids. Bellwood (1985) has stressed that their relatively fair skin and straight black hair set them apart from the Australian Aborigines and the upland inhabitants of New Guinea. He sees these groups in the islands of Southeast Asia as being descended from the Austronesian-speaking people who moved into the area during prehistory, ultimately from southern China.

We now have a new method for tracing the course of such major trends in human expansion, in the form of characteristic genetic mutations that have occurred in the DNA of expanding populations. As Cavalli-Sforza (1991) has shown, there is a general correlation between language and genetics. In the case of the Southern Mongoloids, we find that the languages they speak include Austro-Tai and Austro-Asiatic.

Mitochondrial DNA (mtDNA), a form of DNA that is inherited exclusively from the mother, comprises 16,569 base pairs which encode 13 proteins involved in electron transport and cellular respiration (Stoneking and Wilson 1989). While all mtDNA molecules in an individual appear identical, there are occasions when a part of the sequence mutates or changes; this change is then passed on to the next generation. By evaluating the characteristics of modern mtDNA, it is possible to suggest relationships between widely scattered groups, which are best explained by their sharing a common ancestor. The Asian-specific deletion, for example, has been found in 18 percent of East Asians, in people from Taiwan, Japan, Tonga, and the Philippines. Ballinger and his co-workers (1992) have studied seven Asian populations for their mtDNA sequence variation. They found that all have in common two polymorphisms, pointing to a common ancestry, with the highest frequency being found in the Vietnamese. Again, the occupants of highland New Guinea do not have these genetic markers, but they recur in Pacific and Southeast Asian island populations, as well as among the aboriginal inhabitants of inland Malaysia. These last groups speak languages which fall within the Austro-Asiatic stock.

This information has become available only recently, and its implications are still being absorbed. Initial results, however, support the hypotheses that the New World was colonized across the Bering land bridge, and that some of the peoples of Island Southeast Asia and the Pacific islands originated on the Asian mainland. The high sequence diversity found in Vietnam might also indicate that this coastal region was a source for the expansion of populations. Much more information will become available in due course, but in terms of placing Khok Phanom Di in its broader perspective, the clear possibility that its inhabitants were part of this process of human expansion is posed.

We have seen that the development of sedentism and agriculture strongly favor expansion of numbers. The spread of agricultural communities from the Near East into Europe has been considered recently on the basis of archaeological and genetic data (Ammerman and Cavalli-Sforza 1984). They proposed the wave of advance model to account for a movement in a westerly direction which averaged 25 kilometers per generation. Naturally, this is an average which would have varied with local conditions. Renfrew (1987) has argued that speakers of Indo-European languages originally spread into Europe on a similar time-scale, while Cavalli-Sforza (1991) has shown that there are genetic grounds for an east–west spread of agricultural groups into Europe.

The conjunction of archaeological, linguistic, and genetic data has a long ancestry in Southeast Asia, where the first recorded instance of comparative linguistics in the region occurred in 1603. De Houtman, a Dutch sea captain, noted similarities between the Malay languages and those of Malagasy (Madagascar, Blust 1985:59). Since then, much research has been undertaken on the languages of Southeast Asia, and information relevant to any consideration of the area's prehistory has been obtained. Yet there is much still to be done. Some of the languages remain names on a map, and the pace of change threatens extinctions and the loss of critical information. We must also be cautious in attempting to relate the present distribution of languages to the archaeological record. Languages can become extinct, words can be adopted across considerable distances without population movement, and the pace of linguistic change can be highly variable.

Most linguists recognize three super families of languages in Southeast Asia, known as Austro-Tai, Austro-Asiatic, and Sino-Tibetan. The status of the first remains controversial. Benedict (1942, 1975) has proposed that this is a great linguistic superstock which incorporates Austronesian, Thai, Kadai, and Miao-Yai. On the basis of the large number of shared cognate words, Benedict proposed a genetic relationship between many of the languages spoken in Southeast Asia (Figs. 8.1–3). These Austro-Tai languages all contrast with a second language stock, known as Sino-Tibetan, which includes Tibetan, Karen of eastern Burma, and Chinese. When the Chinese imperial ambitions led them, in the late first millennium B.C., to what is now southern China, they encountered people who spoke Austro-Tai and Austro-Asiatic languages. The latter comprises over 150 languages within three sub-families: Munda, Nicobarese, and Mon-Khmer (Diffloth 1991). Vietnamese and Khmer are the best known of the third sub-family, but less is known of a further member, known as Mon. This is close to Khmer, and was formerly spoken in Central Thailand. However, with the expansion of Thai speakers during the last millennium, Mon now survives in pockets on the margins of the Chao Phraya Valley. Surviving inscriptions from Central Thailand reveal that Mon was the language of the Dvaravati civilization of the first millennium A.D., and most workers agree that this group had local roots. Khmer is the national language of Cambodia, and again, the earliest inscriptions in the lower Mekong Valley include old Khmer texts. Vietnamese has spread during the last millennium from the Red River Valley to coastal Central Vietnam and the Mekong Delta region. This southward spread has led to a considerable reduction in the area where Cham is spoken. The Cham language is Austronesian with close similarities to languages of island Southeast Asia. It was probably introduced into central Vietnam during the first millennium B.C. This

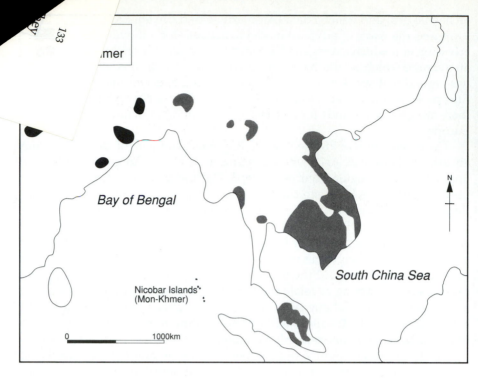

FIGURE 8.1   *The distribution of the Austro-Asiatic languages in Southeast Asia.*

geographic fragmentation of Austro-Asiatic languages is seen elsewhere in what was surely once a broad belt of people belonging to this language family. The second sub-family is now spoken only on the Nicobar Islands, and the third is found in central and eastern India, where it is spoken by about five million Munda people. They are rice cultivators whose distribution is thought to have been reduced by pressure from Indian groups. While stoutly retaining their identity, they live in relatively remote areas.

The widespread distribution of Austro-Asiatic languages must be considered with their considerable diversity. Even Mon Khmer has 12 main branches, and Diffloth has suggested that their differences are compatible with separation as long as at least three to four thousand years ago. This date takes us back to the initial settlement of Khok Phanom Di. At the same time, groups belonging to the Austro-Asiatic language family have been exposed to many intrusions. We have seen how Thai, Indian, and Karen speakers have cut up the distribution of Austro-Asiatic into isolated groups. The Chinese have also had a major impact, particularly in Vietnam, for the northern part of that country was part of the Chinese empire for eight centuries.

The relationship between the Austro-Asiatic and Austro-Tai language families is a matter of considerable relevance to the prehistorian. If, for example, it could be shown that they are related, then we could seek a common origin and early population expansion in association with rice cultivation in

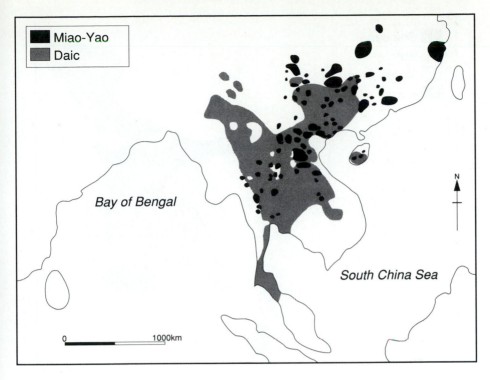

FIGURE 8.2   *The distribution of the Austro-Tai languages in Southeast Asia.*

Southeast Asia and eastern India, in the same way that Renfrew has argued for a conjunction between Indo-European languages and the spread of agriculturalists into Europe. Such a common origin was first proposed by Schmidt in 1906 (Ruhlen 1991), when he linked them into one language stock termed Austric, but it has not been widely adopted. Benedict (1976) has noted that, while the two exhibit a basic similarity in morphology, they do not share a sufficient number of common roots to permit linking them genetically. Benedict (1975:33) has suggested that an extinct Austro-Tai language may have been replaced by Austro-Asiatic, yielding up some of its words in the process. On the other hand, it has to be recognized that languages will, if separated for long enough, diverge so far from each other that no resemblances will remain. The lack of common roots does not, therefore, rule out the possibility that Austro-Asiatic and Austro-Tai languages share an ultimate common ancestor.

Why should we be concerned with the present distribution of languages? Languages change with time and distance, but may also retain elements of a common vocabulary and structure. Therefore, if two languages at the extreme ends of a family's distribution share common cognates, despite a long period of geographic isolation, then they may provide evidence of an early core vocabulary. This vocabulary has been widely used as a means of identifying aspects of early culture that are beyond the scope of archaeological techniques. By tracing such cases, it is possible not only to propose an ancestral vocabulary, which is in itself of considerable interest to prehistorians, but

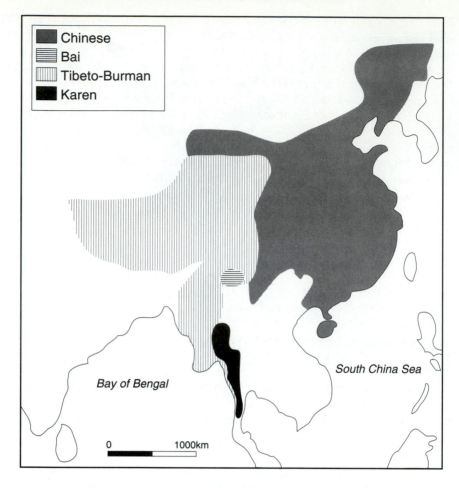

FIGURE 8.3   *The distribution of the Sino-Tibetan languages in Southeast Asia.*

also to establish the expansionary patterns that underlie present language distribution. Again, however, this approach must be followed with due caution. An innovative word in the center of distribution of a language family might spread outwards between linked communities to the periphery, and then be replaced in the core area, leading to erroneous conclusions if uncritically applied. A group of agriculturalists moving into an area where rice has been cultivated and being unfamiliar with it, could apply their own word for grain to the novel plant, or adopt the local word into their own language.

In Southeast Asia, tracing the expansion of peoples through archaeological and linguistic evidence has been most successful for Austronesian, a language family placed in the Austro-Tai super stock by Benedict. This success reflects the fact that Austronesian speakers spread largely by sea and the occupation of coastal fringes or islands. This would have reduced the impact of borrowings and later encroachments which have made the study of Austro-Asiatic linguistic history so difficult. We have seen that a perceptive

Dutchman in the early seventeenth century noted similarities between the language of Malagasy and Malaysia. This similarity is the result of maritime exchange and settlement by Austronesian speakers. Archaeology, linguistics, and biological anthropology have contributed to an understanding of the expansion of Austronesian speakers across an enormous area, from Malagasy to Easter Island. By tracing shared innovations, linguists have identified the island of Formosa, where three remotely related groups of Austronesian speakers survive, as being close to the original homeland. Most would also agree that parts of mainland Southeast Asia must have been occupied once by pre-Austronesian speakers because of the links that have been established with surviving Austro-Tai languages.

Blust (1976) has compared many words found in different Austronesian languages, and through identifying cognate words which probably belong to a proto-language, he has listed a number of activities and artifacts which lay at the origin of the Austronesian expansion. Words can, of course, change their meaning, and this exercise is not without its pitfalls. Dating, too, is not a straightforward exercise, particularly where it takes us back many millennia, Bellwood (1989, 1991), for example, has suggested about 5000 B.C., and a location on the coast of eastern China, for the time and homeland of Proto-Austronesian speakers. The people in question had words for cooked rice, husked rice, rice in the field, and for the domestic pig, chicken, and dog. They had the bow, bamboo fish traps, and made pottery. Weaving was practiced on a loom in villages with dwelling houses raised on posts and entered by a notched log ladder. Roofs were gabled with a ridge pole, and a reed thatch was used. Inside, there were shelves for storing pots. Maritime technology was well advanced, for there are words for an outrigger, bailer, rudder, cross seat, and rollers for beaching a canoe.

Such maritime, agricultural communities lie at the origins of a "wave of advance" that took their descendants first to the Philippines, then following the linguistic trail to the islands and coasts of Papua New Guinea, Indonesia, and Melanesia. The trail, already having many routes, then split further as some groups went west to Malaysia and Malagasy and others to the east. They occupied the island of Fiji, Samoa, and Tonga and then set out in an easterly direction in what surely constitutes the greatest maritime migration in human history, colonizing virtually all the inhabitable islands of Polynesia, reaching South America, Hawaii, and remote Easter Island. From eastern Polynesia, some sailed southwest to reach New Zealand. As they proceeded, they adapted to local conditions. Rice was dropped from the repertoire early as unsuitable habitats were encountered. Pigs reached the tropical Pacific Islands but pottery-making was abandoned. By the time New Zealand was settled, pigs, rice, and pottery were remote memories; taro and yams were introduced to New Zealand, but of domestic animals, only the dog continued, faithful to the end.

The pattern of settlement can be traced archaeologically and linguistically. It seems that when these Austronesian speakers reached Papua and New Guinea, they encountered well-organized local communities, which had been cultivating root crops for many millennia. They skirted the coast of this area. Nor did they settle the mainland coast of what is now China south of the Xijiang River, Vietnam, or Cambodia. At least if they did, they have left no surviving evidence of their language, for the Austronesian Cham language of central Vietnam is the result of a more recent occupation of the area from island Southeast Asia.

It is intriguing to compare the word list for a proto-Austronesian language of mainland China with what archaeologists found at Hemudu, the earliest site in this area that has yielded the remains of cultivated rice. Quite apart from the rice, we find evidence for wooden houses raised on stilts, the domestic dog and pig, as well as evidence for fishing and hunting. Being close to the lakes and the sea, it is hard to overlook the likelihood that these people were also proficient in boat-building. Certainly their houses reveal mastery of carpentry. Hemudu is not the only such site in the area of the lower Yangzi River. Pearson and Underhill (1987:813), for example, have noted that woven fabric has survived at Majiabang to the north.

If the wave of advance from the lower Yangzi followed an island route which involved those who spoke Austronesian, what of the mainland itself? It will be remembered that Austronesian has been found a home in the Austro-Tai language phylum by Benedict. Benedict (1975) has suggested that south China was the center for the dispersal of the mainland Austro-Tai languages. Again, we encounter some most interesting roots that have been constructed for proto-Austro-Tai. These include the words for field, garden, to sow, winnow, the pestle and mortar, to cultivate, seed, grain, and betel (a mild stimulant). Rice agriculture, together with domestic cattle and water buffalo, were central elements in the early Austro-Tai economy, along with sugarcane, and ginger. There are common roots in several of the Austro-Tai languages for rice as a cereal, as a grain, prepared rice, and rice as a meal. There are also common roots for hunting and fishing, bait, the fishhook, trapping fish, and the spear. Proto-Austro-Tai also had words for weaving, to sew, and to plait.

In terms purely of our knowledge of the archaeological record and the present distribution of languages, it is hard to avoid the conclusion that the early rice farming communities of the Yangzi Valley, identified from Pengtoushan to Hemudu, spoke a language ancestral to languages in the Austro-Tai phylum. The distribution of the former is compatible with a mainland riverine spread in a southerly direction from an original center of rice cultivation in the extensive marshlands of the Yangzi Valley. In terms of archaeology, sites that have yielded rice remains tend to be later as one proceeds in a southerly direction. There was also a proliferation of sites in the Yangzi Valley itself. In the middle reaches of the river valley, we find that the early site of Pengtoushan was succeeded by numerous sites of the Daxi culture (4500–3000 B.C.), which in turn developed into the Qujialing culture (3000–2500 B.C.). This extended as far east as Lake Poyang, and the sites have in common large samples of rice, the domestic pig and dog, clay spindle whorls, and cemeteries in which the dead were interred with offerings that included pottery vessels of widespread forms: the ting tripods and pedestaled bowls.

Two rivers provide communication through the southern uplands in the direction of the coast, the Xiangjiang and the Ganjiang. At the confluence of the latter with the Yangzi, we encounter similar rice-cultivating village communities belonging to the Shanbei culture, dated to the third millennium B.C. Chang (1986) has acknowledged the widespread distribution of similar pottery and other artifact forms in the Shanbei and many other regional groupings at this juncture by ascribing them to the Lungshanoid horizon. A most intriguing question is the southernmost limit of settlements which may belong to it. Chang is in no doubt, for example, of the Lungshanoid affiliations of Shixia on the Beijiang River (c. 2500 B.C.). This settlement not only contained a large sample of rice, including offerings in some of the 108 graves excavated, but also the Lungshanoid-style tripods and jade ornaments in the form of rings, beads, and pendants. The assemblage matches very closely those recovered in the Shanbei culture to the north, and along with the nearby site of Niling, is most easily explained as a southward, riverine expansion from the mid-Yangzi area. At this point, since Shixia lies close to the valley of the Xijiang River, and therefore to the coast of southern China, one might expect a proliferation of like sites in this region. But that is not the case. Moreover, it is stressed that it is this southern edge of the Lungshanoid horizon where one encounters the region in which Austro-Asiatic languages are thought to have been spoken.

There is also a fruitful source of information in the survival of words in the languages spoken in parts of southern China today. Norman (1985) for example, has considered the Chinese time cycle, which incorporates a cycle of twelve earthly branches and ten heavenly stems. This was used at the beginning of Chinese history, and the symbols are among the most frequently found graphs on the Shang oracle bones. Norman has found that the names for six of the graphs used to describe animals have an Austro-Asiatic origin, the Chinese forms most closely resembling those in Vietnamese and Muong. Norman and Mei (1976) have further argued, on the basis of loanwords into Chinese, that Austro-Asiatic languages were formerly spoken well into what is now southern China. Thus the word for "to die" in eastern Han China has an Austro-Asiatic origin. Old Chinese words for ivory and tiger, and even the word Chiang for the Yangzi river are said to be Austro-Asiatic. They have also shown that the Austro-Asiatic word for dog, which is present from Assam to Vietnam, was in use in Vietnam during the second century A.D. The Min dialect is spoken in Fujian and northeastern Guangdong, provinces on the southeast coast of China. While most words can be traced back to early Chinese, there are some, such as the words for shaman, child, son, crab, and small fish, which have an Austro-Asiatic origin. Norman and Mei see these as evidence for an early Austro-Asiatic substratum there. Hashimoto (1972) has also studied the languages of southeastern coastal China, and has found words in Cantonese and Min which indicate that Austro-Asiatic languages were once spoken in that region.

There is also the linguistic evidence itself, although less is known of these Austro-Asiatic languages than those of the Austro-Tai stock. Their distribution, incorporating Vietnam, Cambodia, parts of central Thailand, the Nicobar Islands, central Malaysia, Assam (Khasi), Burma, Yunnan (Palaung-Wa), and parts of India, reveal to Diffloth (1991) a separation which must have occurred well back into the prehistoric past. Zide and Zide (1976) have sought common roots in the Munda languages and those of Southeast Asia. They have reconstructed on this basis a proto-Munda language which included words for uncooked, husked rice that match those used in Mon Khmer, Rumai, Khmu, and Lawa to the east. Shared cognates are also found over this huge area for bamboo and bamboo shoots, pestle and mortar, husking rice, to get drunk, the dog, cow, and chicken, and most intriguingly, for copper-bronze. The implication is clear: the ancestral Munda language was related to the languages of people who grew rice and knew of metallurgy, and may well have expanded in a westerly direction from the Austro-Asiatic heart-land in Southeast Asia deep in the prehistoric past. Karen and Thai, two quite distinct non-Austro-Asiatic languages, were then introduced much more re-cently and severed the Munda from their Austro-Asiatic relatives. The distri-bution of these language families, bearing in mind the constant shared cognates for rice and domestic stock in each, therefore suggest that there were three separate expansions of rice agriculturalists, one by sea first to the islands of Southeast Asia, a second which moved south from the Yangzi, a third which originated in the present area of the Austro-Asiatic languages.

This conclusion is borne out by our present understanding of the archae-ological evidence. Meacham, for example, has been prominent in stressing the likelihood of indigenous origins in southern China for the Neolithic communities there (Meacham 1983). He has stressed the importance of the drowned land which would once have stretched up to one hundred miles out across what is now the South China Sea. This area of tide-dominated deltas, mudflats, and mangrove swamps could have sustained a population of sedentary communities that lived off the rich, self-replenishing marine re-sources which we have also encountered at Khok Phanom Di. Meacham has named this drowned country Nanhailand. It is highly significant to find that, as soon as the sea stabilized at a level slightly higher than it is at pre-sent, settlements were established all the way from Taiwan down to central Vietnam. These date back six millennia, and the people in question lived off fish and shellfish, made pottery, and polished stone adzes, used sandstone polishers and on occasion, buried their dead within their settlements. At Tung Shan, for example, located in Hong Kong, the lowest level contained the remains of sand-tempered, cord-marked pottery and flaked stone tools (Qiao Xiaoquin 1991).

Similar coastal sites are known along the coast of Vietnam. Settlements were established soon after the formation of the new, raised coastline. They pose issues of considerable importance in Southeast Asian prehistory. Do they represent maritime communities responding to the rising sea level by relocating their settlements? This seems the most likely explanation for their number and the variety of material culture encountered. There is no evi-dence either in Vietnam or in southern China for a migration of people from anywhere else. While resolution of this issue may have to await the discov-ery of sites under the present shallow sea that overlies the continental shelf, Phong (1985) and Tan (1985) have stressed that the stone-working tradition seen at Cai Beo, Da But, and Quynh Van culture sites matches closely that found in the inland Hoabinhian and Bacsonian rock shelters. Since these lat-ter sites were occupied, with no room for doubt, for at least six millennia be-fore the earliest of these coastal sites, there are strong grounds for proposing a long-term continuity in the settlement of this part of Southeast Asia over the last ten thousand years at least. This could be extended back another eight millennia if we include the Son Vi culture. We also find that the coastal sites made use of netweights, became steadily more proficient at grinding and polishing stone tools, and interred their dead in inhumation cemeteries.

The Vietnamese call these sites Neolithic, but this raises an issue in need of close examination. No evidence has yet been found for the cultivation of rice in these early coastal sites. This may well be the result of insufficient sampling, for sophisticated retrieval techniques must be employed, particularly where rice chaff was not used as a tempering agent in pottery, to recover fragile plant remains. We cannot, however, doubt that there was a dense distribution of these sedentary, coastal groups in southern China and Vietnam. At least two millennia after the establishment of these coastal sites, we encounter the first evidence for inland villages whose inhabitants cultivated rice and raised domestic stock. The best-known group of such sites has been called the Phung Nguyen culture, and they cluster above the confluence of the Red and Black rivers.

Although these sites share an agricultural economy, exchange in exotic goods, and status differentials in inhumation cemeteries, parallels in vessel forms are too vague to encourage us to admit the Phung Nguyen sites to membership in the Lungshanoid horizon. Moreover, Tan (1985) has pointed out that the preferred method of decorating Phung Nguyen pottery involves incised curvilinear bands infilled with comb or shell impressions. He has pointed to parallels with pottery from Samrong Sen in Cambodia and Ban Kao and Non Nok Tha in Thailand. We can now also add to this list the early incised pottery of Ban Chiang and some of the mortuary wares from Khok Phanom Di. Indeed, Khok Phanom Di and Nong Nor are two sites which indicate that this pattern of coastal settlement was also present along the shore of the Gulf of Siam. We remain alone in undertaking research on the pattern of coastal adaptation in this area, however, and have not yet found any site which dates back to the initial establishment of the raised coast. Nevertheless, we have shown that the area was settled by the mid third millennium B.C., and that rice cultivation had been established by 2000 B.C. Moreover, the third and second millennia B.C. in the lowlands of the Red, Mekong, and Chao Phraya rivers, witnessed a great expansion of rice cultivators and proliferation of village sites. We have also found that copper and tin were being smelted by the mid second millennium B.C. in Central Thailand, the Mekong and the Red River valley.

9

Synthesis and Conclusions

The recovery of all this archaeological information began effectively only in the 1960s, and has gathered pace in the last decade. We could advance more than one model to account for what we see in the archaeological record. In essence, we are dealing with a complex issue. Was there a single geographic region which witnessed the domestication of rice, or more than one? In either case, does our present understanding of the archaeological record suggest that the transition to rice farming was followed by a major expansion in the number of people and their spread into an ever-increasing area? A balanced review of this issue must incorporate not only archaeological, human biological, and linguistic information, but also an understanding of how rice may have been converted from a wild marsh grass to a cultivated cereal. We have no sequence of sites in which this transition occurred, quite probably because it took place in the inundated coastal plains. However, one of us has proposed that there were three variables that would have encouraged rice domestication (Higham 1993).

The first is that communities would need to be sedentary, at least during the growing season. This need reflects the simple finding that a field of cultivated rice is a target for any number of predators from birds to deer and pigs, and needs constant protection. The technique for harvesting must also involve cutting the stalk rather than beating the rice into a container, because rice propagates itself by seed shedding when it is ripe. There is, therefore, a fragile connective point which shatters when, for example, the wind disturbs the plant. Harvesting wild rice by beating it into a container mimics a natural process. But sickle-harvesting selects for the rice plants which have undergone a genetic mutation in favor of a tough connective tissue retaining the seed in place. Under natural circumstances, this mutation is not conducive to the plant's propagation. But it is advantageous for human societies, because is is much easier to harvest without losses due to the shattering tendency.

Finally, there must be a satisfactory location for wild or indeed early cultivated rice to flourish near permanent human settlements. While it is unwise to generalize, we know that where rivers tend to break their banks and flood, a common occurrence in monsoon lands, the floodwaters deposit sediment which often forms raised levees. Behind such natural barriers, tributary streams have their access to the main channel blocked, or at least reduced, and their own flooding creates swamplands behind the coastal fringe which are favored habitats for rice. We also know that the temperature during the middle Holocene in the Yangzi Valley was several degrees warmer than it is at present, and the marshlands bordering this great river were very extensive. If rice was not actually domesticated there, then at the least it would have been a most attractive habitat for rice farmers to occupy. We must, therefore, stress that the coastal tract from the mouths of the Yangzi to the Chao Phraya, long since inundated, would have been a likely location of transitions to rice cultivation. If this is accepted, we can now consider various alternative possibilities for the origins and spread of rice farming.

Any models for the origins and expansion of agricultural communities need to take into account the distribution and history of the various languages of Southeast Asia. Tracing the spread of Austronesian languages from a proposed homeland on the Southeast Asian mainland is made relatively straightforward because it involved maritime transport and the occupation of islands. The situation on the mainland, however, is much more difficult, because of the likelihood of movement of people and cross-influences in more than one direction. Bayard (1975) has published a proposed distribution of language families in Southeast Asia during the fourth and possibly the third millennium B.C. (Fig. 9.1). It is important to note that the Chinese languages are firmly placed well north of the Yangzi River, while the Austro-Tai family of languages including proto Thai, Kadai, and Austronesian, are placed in the Yangzi and Xijiang river valleys and the coast of Southeast China. The Austro-Asiatic languages are found from east coastal China and Vietnam to northern Burma and India.

The first model begins with the former coastal marshes which now lie off the Yangzi delta. By the sixth millennium B.C., agricultural communities had occupied the lower and middle valleys of this river, and continued their wave of advance down the rivers towards the south, and offshore to Taiwan and the Philippines. These communities were composed of early Austro-Tai-speaking southern Mongoloid people. Archaeologically, they are seen in the Hemudu, Pengtoushan, Daxi, Qujialing and later Lungshanoid horizon cultures. One branch expanded by sea to the islands of Southeast Asia, and spoke early Austronesian languages. The other remained on the mainland and anticipated the many Austro-Tai languages. In this model, which has only one center of origin for rice domestication, these farmers were to encounter coastal fisher-gatherer groups as they moved south. The two became integrated. Rice farming was adopted by the southern people, who retained their Austro-Asiatic languages, and continued the process of expansion into the Chao Phraya, Mekong and Red River valleys. Ultimately, some groups at the expanding edge of the wave of advance reached as far as western India.

We do not find this model convincing. The deep divide between the Austro-Tai and Austro-Asiatic languages, and the cultural continuity which forms such a strong undercurrent in the prehistoric sequences in coastal

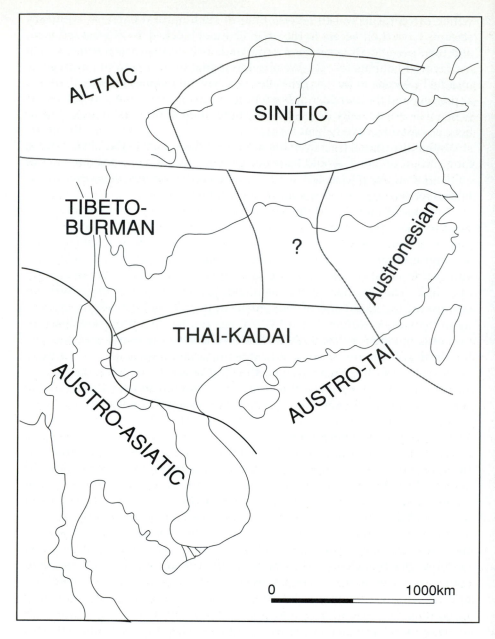

FIGURE 9.1   *The distribution of languages in Southeast Asia during the fourth and possibly the third millennia B.C. (after Bayard 1975).*

regions of southern China and Vietnam, not to mention the inherently unconvincing scene of rice becoming an important part of the diet only after its benefits were made apparent by contact with the expanding peoples of the Lungshanoid horizon, all argue against it.

If Norman and Mei (1976) are correct in placing Austro-Asiatic speakers in the Yangzi Valley and from Fujian south into Guangdong during the late prehistoric period, then it is conceivable that an expansion southward from the Yangzi lakes involved not Austro-Tai but Austro-Asiatic speakers. Ultimately, this wave of advance would have involved settlement of lowlands throughout mainland Southeast Asia and into eastern India and the Nicobar Islands. Could the present Austro-Tai speakers then represent a later and unrelated expansion into the northern part of the Austro-Asiatic area? And if so, where did these people come from, and when? We find this model rather less plausible than that which follows.

The third model begins as does the first, with rice cultivation in the Yangzi Valley. This process involved considerable population growth there, seen in the Daxi, Qujialing, Majiabang, and Shanbei cultures. Some groups moved down the river valleys to the south, but by the third millennium B.C., their progress was slowed by the upland, inhospitable terrain. But there was a further factor. There had been other transitions to rice cultivation in Southeast Asia. The multitude of agricultural communities now known in the middle country of the Red River Valley, along the coast of central Vietnam, in the flatlands flanking the lower and middle Mekong, and in central Thailand reflect a parallel but independent pattern of population growth, which would account for the widespread distribution of Austro-Asiatic languages proposed by Bayard (1975). This model acknowledges the likelihood that the earlier inhabitants of the rock shelters in Southeast Asia might have spoken proto Austro-Asiatic languages, as would those we first encounter in the maritime habitats following the establishment of a coast higher than at present. We note that the abandonment of these rock shelters took place, so far as we can tell, at a time when lowland communities practising rice cultivation were proliferating.

In both the Yangzi and the southern cases, the settlement form and associated evidence for behavior present interesting parallels. The preferred pattern was occupation so as to command low-lying, seasonally flooded land. People lived in villages and pursued a mixed economy of rice cultivation, fishing, raising domestic stock, hunting and collecting. This is a flexible and safe strategy, as may be seen in its robust presence down to the present day. The prehistoric villages did not grow to any appreciable size, a factor in their expansion over such a large area, from the shores of the Gulf of Bac Bo to eastern India. The inhumation cemetery is virtually ubiquitous in such villages, and mortuary rituals involved the interment of the dead with a range of burial goods thought to represent their status and occupation in life. Weaving, pottery-making, fishing, hunting, and, in the southern area, metallurgy, are all encountered. Exchange in exotic goods over considerable distances is also a regular feature, and the results of such contact in terms of similar artifacts and related behavior have been noted by Chang in what he describes as the Chinese Interaction Sphere.

We find this third model of multiple transitions to rice cultivation, and its expansion by speakers of two distinct language families, most plausible. But we must also consider how it might be tested and refined or rejected. We have been at pains to stress that archaeology in Southeast Asia still has a short history and very few sites have been fully reported. If it could be demonstrated that rice was cultivated in the fifth or the fourth millennia B.C.

in the coastal sites of Vietnam, it would sustain this hypothesis. Further fieldwork and the recovery of inland agriculturally based village communities in the Chao Phraya, Mekong, and Red River valleys antedating the earliest Lungshanoid sites in southern China would also lend weight to a southern center of expansion. And this brings us directly to Khok Phanom Di and Nong Nor. At the former, we have clear evidence for rice cultivation in a coastal context by 2000 B.C., and possible palynological evidence much earlier still. Do these sites represent the southern extreme of a process of expansion which originated three millennia earlier in the swamps of the Yangzi Valley? Or are they the result of more local transitions to agriculture which occurred along the broad band of now drowned Sundaland and Nanhailand? We favor the latter alternative, but all must acknowledge the need for further fieldwork to resolve this issue.

REFERENCES

Allen, W. L., and J. B. Richardson.
  1971. The Reconstruction of Kinship from Archaeological Data: The Concepts, the Methods and the Feasibility. *American Antiquity* 36:41–53.

Ammerman, A. J., and L. L. Cavalli-Sforza.
  1984. *The Neolithic Transition and the Genetics of Populations in Europe.* Princeton: Princeton University Press.

Anderson, D. D.
  1990. *Lang Rongrien Rock Shelter, a Pleistocene-Early Holocene Archaeological Site from Krabi, Southwestern Thailand.* University Monograph 71. University Museum, Philadelphia.

Arnold, J. E.
  1991. Transformation of a Regional Economy: Socio-Political Evolution and the Production of Valuables in Southern California. *Antiquity* 65:953–62.

Ballinger, S. W., T. G. Schurr, A. Torroni, Y. Y. Gan, J. A. Hodge, K. Hassan, K. H. Chen, and D. C. Wallace.
  1992. Southeast Asian Mitochondrial DNA Analysis Reveals Genetic Continuity of Ancient Mongoloid Migrations. *Genetics* 130:139–52.

Battaglia, D. B.
  1983. Syndromes of Ceremonial Exchange in the Eastern Calvados: The View from Sabarl Island. In *The Kula. New Perspectives on Massim Exchange,* ed. by J. W. Leach and E. Leach, 445–65. Cambridge: Cambridge University Press.

Bayard, D.T.
  1975. North China, South China, South East Asia, or Simply "Far East"? *Journal of the Hong Kong Archaeological Society* 6:71–9.

———.
  1984. Rank and Wealth at Non Nok Tha: The Mortuary Evidence. Southeast Asian Archaeology at the XV Pacific Science Congress. *Otago University Studies in Prehistoric Anthropology* 16:87–128.

Bellwood, P. S.
  1985. *Prehistory of the Indo-Malaysian Archipelago.* London: Academic Press.

———.
  1989. The Colonization of the Pacific: Some Current Hypotheses. In *The Colonization of the Pacific. A Genetic Trail,* ed. by A. V. S. Hill and S. W. Serjeantson, 1–59. Research Monographs on Human Population Biology no. 7. Oxford: Clarendon Press.

———.
  1991. The Austronesian Dispersal and the Origin of Languages. *Scientific American* 265(1):70–5.

Benedict, P. K.
  1942. Thai, Kadai and Indonesian: A New Alignment in Southeastern Asia. *American Anthropologist* 44: 576–601.

_____.
  1975. *Austro-Thai Language and Culture.* Human Relations Area Files, New Haven.

_____.
  1976. Austro-Thai and Austroasiatic. In *Austroasiatic Studies Part I,* ed. P. N. Jenner, L. C. Thompson, and S. Starosta, 1–36. Oceanic Linguistics Special Publication no. 13.

Blust, R.
  1976. Austronesian Culture History: Some Linguistic Inferences and Their Relations to the Archaeological Record. *World Archaeology* 8:19–43.

_____.
  1985. The Austronesian Homeland. A Linguistic Perspective. *Asian Perspectives* 26:107–17.

Cavalli-Sforza, L. L.
  1991. Genes, People and Language. *Scientific American* 265(5):72–7.

Chang, K-C.
  1986. *The Archaeology of Ancient China,* 4th ed. New Haven: Yale University Press.

Christensen, B., and S. Wium-Anderson.
  1977. Seasonal Growth of Mangroves in Southern Thailand. *Aquatic Botany* 3:281–6.

Deetz, J.
  1968. The Inference of Residence and Descent Rules from Archeological Data. In *New Perspectives in Archaeology,* ed. Binford, S. R., and L. R. Binford, 41–8. Chicago: Aldine.

Delvert, J.
  1961. Le Paysan Cambodgien. *Le Monde d'Outre Mer Passé et Présent.* Première Série no. 10. École Practique des Hautes Études, Sorbonne, Paris.

Diffloth, G.
  1991. Austro-Asiatic Languages. *Encyclopaedia Britannica Macropaedia* 22:719–21.

Domrös, M. and P. Gongbing.
  1988. *The Climate of China.* Berlin: Springer-Verlag.

Dove, R. M.
  1980. *Swidden Agriculture in Indonesia. The Subsistence Strategies of the Kalimantan Kantu.* The Hague: Mouton.

Gorman, C. F.
  1977. *A Priori* Models and Thai Prehistory: A Reconsideration of the Beginnings of Agriculture in Southeast Asia. In *Origins of Agriculture,* ed. C. A. Reed, 321–55. The Hague: Mouton.

Hanks, L. M.
  1972. *Rice and Man. Agricultural Ecology in Southeast Asia.* Chicago and New York: Aldine.

Harlan, J.
  1989. Wild-Grass Seed Harvesting in the Sahara and Sub-Sahara of Africa. In *Foraging and Farming. The Evolution of Plant Exploitation,* ed. D. R. Harris and G. C. Hillman, 79–98. London: Unwin Hyman.

Hashimoto, O. Y.
  1972. *Studies in Yue Dialects 1: Phonology of Cantonese.* Cambridge: Cambridge University Press.

Heine-Geldern, R.
  1932. Urheimat und früheste Wanderungen der Austronesier. *Anthropos* 27:543–619

Heald, E. J., and W. E. Odum.
  1971. The Contribution of Mangrove Swamps to Florida Fisheries. *Proceedings of the Gulf and Caribbean Fisheries Institute*. 22:130–5.

Higham, C. F. W.
  1993. The Transition to Rice Cultivation in Southeast Asia. In *The Transition to Agriculture*, in press, ed. T. D. Price and A-B. Gebauer. Santa Fé: School of American Research.

Higham, C. F. W. and A. Kijngam.
  1984. The Mortuary Ritual and its Implications. In *Prehistoric Research in Northeast Thailand*, ed. C. F. W. Higham and A. Kijngam, 413–545. British Archaeological Reports, International Series 231(ii).

Higham, T. F. G.
  1993. The Shell Knives from Khok Phanom Di. In *The Excavation of Khok Phanom Di, Volume III. The Material Culture (Part 1)*, ed. C. F. W. Higham and R. Thosarat, Research Report of the Society of Antiquaries of London, London.

Ho, C-M.
  1984. *The Pottery of Kok Charoen and its Farther Context*. Ph.D. dissertation, University of London.

Houghton, P.
  1975. The Bony Imprint of Pregnancy. *Bulletin of the New York Academy of Medicine* 51:655–61.

Irwin, G. J.
  1983. Chieftainship, Kula, and Trade in Massim Prehistory. In *The Kula. New Perspectives on Massim Exchange*, ed. J. W. Leach and E. Leach, 29–72. Cambridge: Cambridge University Press.

Jones, R. and B. Meehan.
  1989. Plant Foods of the Gidjingali: Ethnographic and Archaeological Perspectives from Northern Australia on Tuber and Seed Exploitation. In *Foraging and Farming. The Evolution of Plant Exploitation*, ed. D. R. Harris and G. C. Hillman, 120–35. London: Unwin Hyman.

Leach, E. R.
  1954. *The Political Systems of Highland Burma*. Cambridge, Mass.: Harvard University Press.

——.
  1961. *Pul Eliya*. Cambridge: Cambridge University Press.

——.
  1973. Concluding address. In *The Explanation of Culture Change*, ed. A. C. Renfrew, 761–71. London: Duckworth.

Lepowsky, M.
  1983. Sudest Island and the Louisade Archipelago in Massim Exchange. In *The Kula. New Perspectives on Massim Exchange*, ed. J. W Leach and E. Leach, 467–501. Cambridge: Cambridge University Press.

Maloney, B. K.
  1991. Palaeoenvironments of Khok Phanom Di: The Pollen, Pteridophyte Spore and Microscopic Charcoal Record. In *The Excavation of Khok Phanom Di, a Prehistoric Site in Central Thailand. Volume II: The Biological Remains (Part I)*, ed. C. F. W. Higham and R. Bannanurag, 7–134. Reports of the Research Committee of the Society of Antiquaries of London no. XLVII, Society of Antiquaries of London and Thames and Hudson.

MacDonald, W. G.
   1978. The Bang Site, Thailand. An Alternative Analysis. *Asian Perspectives* 21(1)
   30–51.

Maschner, H. D. G.
   1991. The Emergence of Cultural Complexity on the Northern Northwest Coast.
   Antiquity 65(249):924–34.

Mansuy, H.
   1923. Résultats des Nouvelles Recherches Effectués sur le Gisement Préhistorique
   de Samrong Sen. *Mémoires du Societé Géologique del Indochine* xi(1).

Meehan, B.
   1982. *Shell Bed to Shell Midden.* Australian Institute of Aboriginal Studies, Canberra.

Meacham, W.
   1983. Origins and Development of the Yüeh Coastal Neolithic: A Microcosm of Culture Change on the Mainland of Southeast Asia. In *The Origins of Chinese Civilization,* ed. D. N. Keightley, 147–75. Berkeley: University of California Press.

Mouhot, H.
   1864. *Travels in the Central Parts of Indo-China (Siam), Cambodia and Laos.* 2 vols. London: J. Murray.

Norman, J.
   1985. A Note on the Chinese Duodenary Cycle. In *Linguistics of the Sino-Tibetan
   Area: The State of the Art,* ed. G. Thurgood, J. A. Matisoff, and D. Bradley.
   Pacific Linguistics Series C no. 87, 85–9. Department of Linguistics, Research
   School of Pacific Studies, Australian National University.

Norman, J., and T. Mei.
   1976. The Austroasiatics in Ancient South China: Some Lexical Evidence. *Monu-
   menta Serica* 32:274–301.

Odum, E. P.
   1971. *Fundamentals of Ecology.* Philadelphia: W. B. Saunders.

Pearson, R., and A. Underhill.
   1987. The Chinese Neolithic: Recent Trends in Research. *American Anthropologist*
   89:807–22.

Phong, N. T.
   1985. Some Archaeological Questions of the Northern Vietnamese Coastal Areas
   in Relation to Austronesian Origins. *Asian Persectives* 26(1):147–52.

Pietrusewsky, M.
   1984. Pioneers on the Khorat Plateau: The Prehistoric Inhabitants of Ban Chiang.
   Journal of the Hong Kong Archaeological Society 10:90–106.

Pigott, V. C.
   1985. Pre-Industrial Mineral Exploitation and Metal Production in Thailand. *MASCA
   Journal* 3(5):170–4.

Pigott, V. C., and S. Natapintu.
   1988. Archaeological Investigations into Prehistoric Copper Production: The Thailand Archaeometallurgy Project 1984–6. In *The Beginning of the Use of Metals
   and Alloys,* ed. R. Maddin, 156–62. Cambridge Mass.: MIT Press.

Pisnupong, P.
   1981. *The Excavation of Khok Phutsaa.* Fine Arts Department Report, Bangkok.

Qiao Xiaoquin.
   1991. The Adaptation and Communication of the Prehistoric People of Coastal
   South China. Paper read at the Conference on the South China Sea and Adjacent Area, June 1991, Quangzhou, Shenzen, Hong Kong.

Renfrew, A. C.
1987. *Archaeology and Language. The Puzzle of Indo-European Origins.* London: Penguin.

Ruhlen, M.
1991. *A Guide to the World's Languages.* Vol. 1, *Classification.* London: Edward Arnold.

Russel-Hunter, W. D.
1970. *Aquatic Productivity.* New York: Macmillan.

Sonquiao, Z.
1986. *Physical Geography of China.* New York: Wiley.

Sørensen, P., and T. Hatting.
1967. *Archaeological Investigations in Thailand.* Vol. II, *Ban Kao, Part 1: The Archaeological Materials from the Burials.* Copenhagen: Munksgard.

Steeves, T. A.
1952. Wild Rice—Indian Food and a Modern Delicacy. *Economic Botany* 26:107–42.

Stoneking, M., and A. C. Wilson.
1989. Mitochondrial DNA. In *The Colonization of the Pacific. A Genetic Trail,* ed. A. V. S. Hill and S. W. Serjeantson, 215–45. Research Monographs on Human Population Biology, no. 7. Oxford: Clarendon Press.

Tan, H. V.
1985. Prehistoric Pottery in Viet Nam and Its Relationships with Southeast Asia. *Asian Perspectives* 26(1):135–46.

Tayles, N.
1992. *The People of Khok Phanom Di. Health as Evidence of Adaptation in a Prehistoric Southeast Asian Population.* Ph.D. dissertation, University of Otago, New Zealand.

Thompson, J.
1992. *Archaeobotanical Investigations at Phanom Di, Thailand.* Ph.D. dissertation, Australian National University, Canberra, Australia.

Thosarat R.
1989. *Khok Phanom Di and Its Socio-Cultural Implications.* Ph.D. Dissertation, University of Otago.

Turner, G. G. II.
1987. Late Pleistocene and Holocene Population History of East Asia Based on Dental Variation. *American Journal of Physical Anthropology* 73:305–21.

Watson, W.
1979. Kok Charoen and the Early Metal Age in Central Thailand. In *Early South East Asia,* ed. R. B. Smith and W. Watson, 53–62. Oxford: Oxford University Press.

———.
1983. Pre-Han Communication from West China to Thailand. Paper prepared for CISHAAN, Tokyo, September 1983.

Whitten, A. J., S. J. Damanik, J. Anwar, and N. Hisyam.
1984. *The Ecology of Sumatra.* Yogyakarta: Gadjah Mada University Press.

Wu, W-T.
1983 Holocene Palaeogeography Along the Hangzhou Bay on the Basis of Neolithic Cultural Remains. *Acta Geographica Sinica* 38(2):113–27.

Yen, D. E.
1977. Hoabinhian Horticulture: The Evidence and the Questions from Northeast Thailand. In *Sunda and Sahul,* ed. J. Allen, J. Golson, and R. Jones, 556–99. New York and London: Academic Press.

Zhao, S., and W-T. Wu.
   1988. Early Neolithic Hemudu Culture Along the Hangzhou Estuary and the Origin of Domestic Paddy Rice in China. *Asian Perspectives* 27(1):29–34.

Zide, A. R. K., and N. H. Zide.
   1976. Proto-Munda Cultural Vocabulary: Evidence for Early Agriculture. In *Austroasiatic Studies Part I*, ed. P. N. Jenner, L. C. Thompson, and S. Starosta, Oceanic Linguistics Special Publication no. 13:1295–1334.

Index

DATE